Hatha Yoga

Inspirations from a Master

Lectures by Swami Vishnudevananda

Published by
International Sivananda Yoga Vedanta Centre
Headquarters, Sivananda Yoga Ashram
Founder: Swami Vishnudevananda

673 8th Avenue,Val Morin, Quebec, J0T 2R0 Canada
www.sivananda.org

ISBN: 978-81-19394-32-6

Also available at
MOTILAL BANARSIDASS INTERNATIONAL
41 U.A. Bungalow Road, (Back Lane) Jawahar Nagar, Delhi - 110 007
4261 (basement) Lane #3,Ansari Road, Darya Ganj, New Delhi - 110 002
203 Royapettah High Road, Mylapore, Chennai - 600 004
12/1A, 2nd Floor, Bankim Chatterjee Street, Kolkata - 700 073
Stockist : Motilal Books, Ashok Rajpath, Near Kali Mandir, Patna - 800 004

Printed & Bound by
MOTILAL BANARSIDASS INTERNATIONAL

MOTILAL BANARSIDASS
INTERNATIONAL
DELHI

Dedicated to H.H. Sri Swami Sivananda (1887-1963)

Contents

PREFACE

"I went to my Master Swami Sivananda when I was 17 years old. I had not learned yoga from anybody. My Master Sivananda did not teach me, he just touched me and opened my subconscious mind. From my past life all the yogic knowledge came back to me. Of course, *The Complete Illustrated Book of Yoga* was written in this life. But none of these things was ever taught to me by my Master nor any being here on the earth. My Master opened my memory of past lives."

These are Swami Vishnudevananda's own words about his yogic training in the Ashram of Swami Sivananda in Rishikesh in the Himalayas.

In 1957, Swami Sivananda sent his young disciple to take yoga beyond the shores of India: "Go to the West. People are waiting."

For over three decades, Swami Vishnudevananda traveled far and wide. He founded the Sivananda Yoga Vedanta Centers, with many branches both in the West and in India.

The lectures which are presented in this book were recorded in many countries, in public halls, during group meditations (satsaṅgs), in Teachers' Training Courses and symposia.

These inspiring live teachings expand the practical aspects of haṭha yoga which Swami Vishnudevananda himself taught to people all over the world.

A comprehensive introduction to haṭha yoga and meditation can be found in *The Complete Illustrated Book of Yoga* and *Meditation and Mantras,* the two best-selling books written by Swami Vishnudevananda.

The depth of the yogic teachings lies in the fact that they can be experienced through one's own practice. Especially the graduates of the Sivananda Yoga Teachers' Training Course will find this reading easy and uplifting, as it relates very closely to their training experience.

Note of Thanks

We are grateful to the many dedicated members of the Sivananda Centers who preserved and digitalized the tape recordings and created the Swami Vishnudevananda Audio Archives on the internet:

https://audioarchive.sivananda.eu/.

We thank all those who have transcribed the audio recordings and assisted in editing the precious texts of this book.

July 2023
Sivananda Ashram Yoga Camp Headquarters,
Val Morin, Quebec, Canada

INVOCATION

DHYĀNA SLOKAS[1]

First, we invoke the supreme wavelength of OM. There are many obstacles which we must face in our physical and mental circumstances. To elevate yourself to a higher state, you need the grace of God. For this reason, you invoke the same supreme energy of OM in the form of Gaṇeśa. Gaṇeśa is not a different god. Just like water exists as liquid, steam, or ice, so also the same Supreme Being manifests in different names and forms. When you add a little sugar and lemon to pure water, it becomes lemonade. It not only quenches the thirst, which is done by the water, but it is also tasty. In this analogy, the taste corresponds to what is called the qualified brahman or the qualified Absolute. We need this qualified brahman, which has name and form. It allows to add your emotions, your devotion. So, when you pray and repeat Om Śrī Ganapataye Namaḥ, Om Śrī Gaṇeśaya Namaḥ, you are invoking the first deity, the first wavelength, in order to remove obstacles.

1. Verses for Meditation

Gajānanaṃ bhūta gaṇādi sevitam
Kapittha jambū phala sāra bhakṣitam
Umā sutaṃ śoka vināśa kāraṇam
Namāmi vighneśvara pāda paṅkajam

I prostrate before the lotus feet of Gaṇeśa (Vighneśvara), the son of Umā, the cause of destruction of sorrow, who is served by the host of angels (Bhūta-Ganas), who has the face of an elephant and who partakes of the essence of Kapittha and Jambū fruits.

Gaṇeśa is the remover of obstacles and manifests as the son of Lord Śiva. This is not the ordinary meaning of son. God has no son or wife; these are just wavelengths. It means that the powerful energy of OM changes into a qualified energy called Gaṇeśa or Ganapati. The face of an elephant symbolizes a pure intellect.

Then the same universal Śiva aspect changes into the power aspect called Lord of War. This does not relate to ordinary fighting. Lord of the War means Lord of Angels. He helps us to fight our lower energies within our heart, such as lust, anger, greed, hatred, and jealousy. Therefore, we invoke the power aspect of the Supreme Being as Subrahmaṇya, Śaravaṇabhava, Kārtikeya, etc.

Ṣaḍānanaṃ kuṅkuma rakta varṇam
Mahāmatim divya mayūra vāhanam
Rudrasya sūnuṃ surasainya nātham
Guhaṃ sadā'haṃ śaraṇaṃ prapadye

I always take refuge in Guha of six faces (Subrahmaṇya), who is a deep red colour like Kuṅkuma, who possesses great knowledge, who rides the divine peacock, who is the son of Rudra (Śiva), and who is the leader of the army of the gods, angels (Devas).

Next, we invoke the Sarasvatī aspect, the goddess of pure knowledge, symbolized by pure white dress and being seated in a white lotus. Sarasvatī symbolizes purity, goodness, and pure knowledge; playing the musical instrument vīṇā symbolizes pure sound. That pure sound manifests as various types of languages and various types of music. In one hand she is holding a book which represents our knowledge in the physical universe.

Yā kundendu tuṣāra hāra dhavalā
Yā śubhra vastrāvṛtā
Yā vīṇā vara daṇḍa maṇḍita karā
Yā śveta padmāsanā
Yā brahmācyuta śaṅkaraḥ prabhṛtibhir
Devais sadā pūjitā
Sāmāṃ pātu sarasvatī bhagavatī
Niśśeṣa jāḍyāpahā

May the Goddess Sarasvatī, who wears a white garland like the Kunda flower, the moon, and the snow, who is adorned with pure white clothes, whose hands are ornamented with the vīṇā and the gesture of blessings, who is seated on a white lotus, who is always worshipped by Brahmā, Viṣṇu, Śiva and other gods, and who is the remover of all inertness and laziness, protect me.

Then you invoke the blessing of your teacher. Whatever knowledge you seek, it must come through the guru. You may have heard from the autobiography of Gurudev Swami Sivananda how God came to him in the form of the

Untouchable. When he was still a young brahmin boy, Swami Sivananda went and prostrated to a teacher who taught him a martial art, fencing. This is also an art of God, it is knowledge. In the highest tradition it is understood that knowledge is there within you, but it must be ignited by someone. Whoever ignites it is your guru, whether it is knowledge about chemistry, physics, carpentry, or cooking. The guru ignites the knowledge within "I am That I am", "Aham Brahmā Asmi". That guru is Brahmā, the creator, Viṣṇu, the preserver, and Maheśvara, or Śiva, the destroyer.

Gururbrahmā gururviṣṇuḥ
gururdevo maheśvaraḥ
Gurussākṣāt paraṃ brahma
tasmai śrīgurave namaḥ

Prostrations to that Śrī Guru, who is himself the gods Brahmā, Viṣṇu and Maheśvara, and who is verily the Supreme Absolute itself.

Just like water comes from the ocean or the lakes through a tap into your house, – in the same way the supreme knowledge which is within you must be tapped by the channel of devotion. That channel is called the guru. Eventually you realize that there is no difference between guru and disciple. That difference is only an upādhi (veil). In the higher stage, even that upādhi will melt away. But you must have devotion, otherwise your ego will build up. Then knowledge becomes a hindrance to your progress. I am not talking of the highest knowledge, Aham, "I am", but the knowledge we use through the intellect. That knowledge can create further egoism: "I know more, I am a PhD, I am a professor, I am a vedantin,

I am a kuṇḍalinī yogi, I know more rāja yoga, I know more kuṇḍalinī yoga, I know more haṭha yoga." Even that knowledge can bring up a little ego which will stop your progress.

That is why devotion to the guru is prescribed. No guru will make a student a servant or a slave. When the student obeys the guru, it is only for his own benefit, as it removes the little ego. That is the only purpose behind it. A true teacher sees brahman in himself, and he sees also brahman in the student. So, a teacher will not act as a supreme all knowing, all prevailing, omniscient God. He tries to remove his own ego too. If the ego is not removed, then the guru cannot see God in the disciple, nor can he see the same God in the teachings. Then he is not a guru. Then the disciple will not be obedient. Then the knowledge will not be received for the purpose of breaking the ego by removing the upādhis, the identification with the physical body and the mental body or intellectual body.

Thus, invoking the surrender to the guru is the fourth step.

FOUNDATIONS

YOGA AND THE TRIANGLE OF LIFE

The first important question out of which yoga philosophy is evolving is the question: Who am I? This question can only be answered when we discuss two other questions: Where do I come from? Where do I go? This "I", the personality, does not only exist in the present state. It also exists in the past and in the future. This past does not only include this life, but also the time before we were born. How far back? In which condition did this "I" exist in the past? And where will you go after death? The physical body will die, it will go back to the food chain. The body, the central nervous system, the eyes and ears will be eaten away by worms and germs. It becomes the food for plants and vegetables.

Who am I? Where do I come from? Where do I go? These are the three main questions. They can be better understood if we look at life as a triangle. In the West, no matter how much you are scientifically advanced, you only understand life as a straight line. This line begins with birth (A) and ends with death (B). You don't consider that there is something before your birth. Most people do not believe in past or future lives. Even if they believe in a future life, they have a very vague idea, living somewhere with God, somewhere up in the heaven and flying around like angels with wings. There is no clear definition about the afterlife. You think that you are born because of your parents. Then you grow, you perform various activities and reach your favorite position with money, children and grandchildren. Then you sit in a wheelchair, and you die. Life ends.

But yoga is discussing life in a different way: you have an outer experience defined by the five senses, which are seeing, hearing, touching, smelling, and tasting. But when you sit in darkness with eyes closed for five minutes, you shut off the sense world. Now you cannot see, hear, touch, smell, or taste, you have an inner experience. You are not dead because you cannot see the outside world. You are alive, you are an individual personality. That experience of "I" cannot be destroyed because you shut off your five senses. You are aware, you have an awareness that you exist.

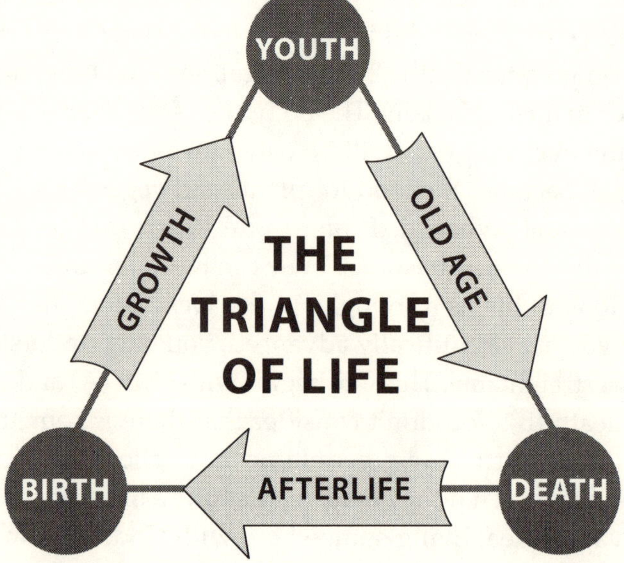

Even if you are blind, you can feel that "I am". Even if you do not remember your name, you will still feel that "I am". This "I" does not need a name, nor qualities or personality to survive. It is pure consciousness, not intellectual consciousness. Pure consciousness is awareness without a name, a form or a quality. That "I" is called Soul or Spirit. While this "I" does not change, body and mind do undergo unavoidable changes described in yoga as "the Triangle of Life".

The Afterlife

Life does not stop at death, because your physical body is gone. Life only changes because you have now a different body, the astral body, without the physical body. That is life hereafter, the bottom line from death (C) back to birth (A). There are several dimensions in the afterlife. According to our mental evolution, we go to different dimensions after death. Dimensions are planes of thought. Depending on the purity and the concentration of your thought, you will go to a higher plane. The astral life is an energy life. We spend the energy for enjoyment there: for example, if you want food, food will come to you by mere thought. If you want a certain type of clothes to wear, your thought will bring them just like in a dream. In dream there is no physical food. But you can get hungry in dream too. And dream hunger can only be appeased by dream food. Just like in the dream your mind creates all the objects for you, so also in the astral plane your mind creates all the things by mere thought.

Here my words are translated. But in the astral world, no matter whether your language in your physical life was German, French, English or Hindi, you do not need a translator. How will you communicate? Telepathically. You see the thought and you transfer the thought. In this energy world, depending on your purity and goodness, you will go to higher dimensions and may live there for thousands of years. Death exists only on the physical plane. In the astral world there is no death. The energy is just slowly weakening. It is running low like a battery until you cannot anymore create the energy necessary for running your instruments. Then you take a birth again here in the physical body.

Again, from Birth (A) to the youthful stage (B), then gradual decline until the death of the physical body (C) and again through the astral existence to rebirth (A). This is called the triangle of life. In the first point (A) we have taken birth in a physical body and on the physical plane to particular parents, in a particular space and time. Why were we born to these particular parents? Do we choose them or are we born to our parents just by accident? Some people are born in an upper-class family, some to a royal family and some are born in Brooklyn in a drug addicted family. Some babies are born in an Ethiopian family, they are just born there to die of hunger. Some people are born with AIDS, because the parents had AIDs. Some people have certain deformities because the mother took a certain kind of medical drugs which created such side-effects for the baby. What is the cause of all this, is it all caused by God? Did God cause one child to be born in a royal family and another child to be born in a starving Ethiopian family to die? Where is justice in that? It is called Karma. According to your past life, your past earthly existence, you have accumulated good or bad karma.

Karma – action and reaction

In traditional India, a potter needs to turn the pottery wheel manually until it reaches a speed of about 2000 – 3000 revolutions per minute (rpm). Then he can use his hands to mold the clay into the required shape. But the wheel will not go on revolving forever, it will slowly go down to 2000r pm, then 1000, then 500, until the clay cannot be molded anymore. Then the potter needs to use his hands to increase the speed again. Similarly, in the physical plane, you create the rpm of your life, positive or negative. Through good actions your thoughts are at a very pure level. Through meditation, yogis increase these rpm even further to a very high speed. After physical death it will take a long time to slow down these rpm. Depending on the speed you will be in higher or lower dimensions.

Once the good karma which you created in the past life is exhausted in the astral plane, you are again born with a new body, depending on where you left in the past life. Suppose you were making a big pot during the last life, and you didn't complete that big pot, then in this life you make the same pot from past memory, from the subconscious memory. This is called habit and is true whether you were engineers, doctors, yogis, philosophers, beggars, drug addicts or alcoholics. If you were an engineer in past life, you will be again an engineer, you will be born in a family suitable for your evolution. If in the last life you were a drug addict, then you will be born in a family where drugs are important. Suppose in the past life a person destroyed several children's life by selling them drugs, then the karma is very bad. The person may then be born in the womb of a mother who is a drug addict. In the womb, the baby will receive blood from the mother, who is herself taking drugs. So, the baby is born as a drug addict. Many children in the

US are born in this way and they suffer terribly because of their parents. This is called law of karma.

Knowledge from Past Lives

Some children excel in playing the piano or the violin in a famous concert hall in Vienna when they are only 5 or 6 years old. Where do these children learn all this? In their past life they were excellent musicians and wanted to play in the Vienna concert hall. But before reaching the required level they died. Will all the knowledge they learned just be wasted and they cannot play anymore, because their physical body dropped off? In the next life, they remember their musical talent from the very beginning. In the same way some people are experts in computers. They were top scientists in their past life. From the beginning they understand any electronic gadget. There are cases in America where children knew how to hack into a bank and transfer millions of dollars to Switzerland. They were even able to penetrate the Pentagon computers. Even the specialists who created all these computers do not understand how these children could decode these programs.

I went to my Master Swami Sivananda when I was 17 years old. I had not learned yoga from anybody. My Master Sivananda did not teach me, he just touched me and opened my subconscious mind. From my past life all the yogic knowledge came back to me. Of course, *The Complete Illustrated Book of Yoga* was written in this life. But none of these things was ever taught to me by my master nor any being here on the earth. My Master opened my memory of past lives.

Many people in the West think that we are born with a blank mind. But what I am trying to tell you is that we are not born equally. We have the experience from the past. Birth is not a blank situation. We are born in a particular family, place, or country with particular thought waves. Astrology is not going to control your life, but that particular astrological sign under which you are born corresponds to the karma which is going to unfold in this life. You may become the chancellor of Austria or the King of England. You can be born in an Indian family as a yogi or you can be born in America, Europe, or Austria, and become a yogi. This is actually happening. I sent swamis to teach in our ashram in India, although they were born in the USA, Austria, Germany, or South America. Or see the example of Swami Ramananda. She was born in Austria and was my first student in 1958 in Canada. After several years I sent her to New York and then back to Austria, where she started the first Sivananda Yoga Vedanta Center in Vienna. From there she then moved to other places.

The Wheel of Birth and Death

Wherever you were born, what was the first thing you all did? You all cried, and the cry is the same in Austria or in India. It is universal. Were any of your babies born happy? We all cried. Why? According to yogic philosophy, before you die, you go through a complete life review. In the same way, just before birth, the baby in the womb will get a flashback of the past life. It will get frightened. It is like coming back into a dungeon. From your transcendental higher level of the astral world, you must return to the physical level, into a baby body. But the baby cannot express any of this. It only cries. The baby prays to God and says: next time I am going to be a yogi. I will meditate and overcome all problems. But this may take several births. Because each time you make this promise, as soon as you are born, there is amnesia. You don't remember anything of the past. You think you are just born for the first time because of that loss of memory.

The catabolic process is increased every day by eating and drinking. Slowly the decay process increases. By age 45–50 it accelerates; then the liver, the heart and other organs do not function properly anymore. The muscles becoming weaker, life is getting dimmer and dimmer, just like a battery which is running out of energy. Then you die. But life does not end here. With the energy created by your thoughts during your physical life, you move to the astral level. When the energy in the astral world runs out you are born again. Through the anabolic process you grow and get youthful and strong. Through the catabolic process you get old and again you die. This goes on forever, it never stops. Until in one life you say: that is sufficient. I want to know who I am. What is this race? Where do I come from? Where do I go? Why do I have problems? Why am I suffering? Why can I not fulfill all my desires? Is there any way I can escape from all this?

Yes, you can close your eyes and stop the thought waves. That is called "*yoga's-citta-vṛtti-nirodhaḥ*" – "yoga is the suspension of the thought waves". When the thought waves slow down, the anabolic process increases. It balances the catabolic process. The heart rate slows down, your mind becomes calm, and you enter the silence. The power of silence is all blissful. Knowledge, the knower and the known become one. Experience, the experiencer and what is experienced become one. This is the goal of life, there is no birth after that. No more time, space, and causation. I am everything, everything is in me. All these past lives are just like a passing dream. I am neither born nor do I die. Birth and death are like a dream, but I am real. Who am I? I am That I am. I am existence, knowledge, and bliss. That is the end of the journey.

If you understand this philosophy, it shows that you already have some experience from this in the past. If you didn't understand it, your life will be an action and reaction life, following the endless chain of cause and effect. So according to your evolution you take yoga, your inner life seriously. You should take it seriously. "How can I reach this transcendental state in this life?" Apply the five points of yoga: proper exercise or āsanas, proper breathing to control the vital energy in the astral body, proper relaxation to balance the energy level, a proper vegetarian diet and positive thinking and meditation. These 5 aspects give you a practical way to reach this state.

Yoga – a Practical Approach

Yoga is not a theory; it is a practice. You practice āsanas or postures to awaken your body. You learn to reduce the catabolic decay process and reach a youthful life even at the age of 80. The āsanas are also practiced to harmonize your astral body. The physical and the astral body are interrelated. If there is resistance in the physical nervous system, the flow of prāṇa (vital energy) is cut off to both the physical and astral bodies.

In acupuncture, needles are used to reduce the resistance in the nervous system. Suppose the prāṇa is not going to the liver, then the acupuncture needle can stimulate that particular meridian. In anatomy we call it a nerve; in yoga it is called a nāḍi. But nāḍis or meridians are not in the physical body. They are in the astral or energy body. By reducing the resistance in the nervous system, the physical body improves, as it can now receive energy from the astral body. Yogis are doing this with the āsanas. Each āsana works on an acupuncture area, each exercise works on a particular meridian. This is how the resistance is reduced. So, āsanas are not just physical exercises. They increase the energy flow from the astral to the physical.

Pranayama, or proper breathing, applies to the nervous system, the left and right hemisphere of the brain. The left hemisphere is analytical, mathematical and action orientated. The right hemisphere is intuitional, emotional, philosophical, musical and artistic. The Western mind works more with the left hemisphere because of its scientific, analytical, and mathematical approach. When the left hemisphere becomes active it inhibits the right hemisphere. Einstein resolved mathematical problems by using the left brain and then went sailing to relax to relax the right brain. He used the intellect guided by intuition. In yoga this corresponds to the ida nāḍi (left) and pingala nāḍi (right). When these two energies are balanced through prāṇāyāma, then the sushumna nāḍi or the central nāḍi or astral channel with the seven cakras is activated. Each cakra corresponds to a higher plane or dimension. According to the evolution of these cakras, we will be born in a particular dimension. You must have heard of the expression "the seventh heaven". Each heaven represents a particular vibratory level.

Through proper relaxation, the energy flow in the nerves and meridians becomes very smooth. Through proper vegetarian diet you can reduce the catabolic activity, instead of increasing it through the consumption of alcohol and drugs. In meditation the mind is turned inward. In deep meditation you find the answer to the Whom am I question: I am That I am. But there are no words to express this. When a sleeping person is asked: are you sleeping, will there be a reply: Yes I am sleeping? Then you know that the person is not sleeping. Similarly in deep meditation, there is no awareness of time, space, or causation. There is no sense of meaning or understanding. Therefore, there are no words to explain it. It is called samadhi. Even if it sounds quite far away, this is your goal. Start with the physical body, reduce the catabolic process by āsanas and prāṇāyāma and increase your youthful life from 18 all the way to 80. Then balance your life through proper diet and practice meditation. Then you will be in that state.

THE FOOD SHEATH

The physical sheath, the food sheath is this body which is made of ice cream, pizza, and bananas. The body is a combination of various elements which we eat. We cannot hold it for a long time because we have borrowed it from the various plants or animals which we ate. Therefore, it is called the food sheath. Eventually it will decompose to take on a new life form.

I am eating tomatoes and my body grows like a tomato. Then I die. Someone puts this body under the earth and plants a tomato plant over it. Then this body becomes a tomato. What are you eating then? You are eating Swami Viṣṇu, but you call it tomato. The body is just tomato, pizza, ice cream, bananas, and hamburgers. Depending on your diet, by the end of your life, several cows and pigs went into this body. That existence which you call this body, cannot be your real existence. Death is only for the physical body which is made up of food. It came from the food chain; it belongs to the food chain and it must go back into the food chain. That is a law. You cannot hold the body for a long time because other animals and living creatures are waiting. Your body is being recycled. If the body is the real "I", then the "I" is finite. But within me I know that I cannot be a finite being. If that would be so, then why would I search for the answer to the question "who am I"?

Do not identify with the wrong thing. The body is not the soul. You are not a finite mortal. "I am," means not this body. I have learned one thing: I am not at all perfect. I am 60 now, going to be 61. It took 60 years to learn that I am not perfect yet. Only when you transcend this body, this cage, then you know that you are perfect. As long as you are identifying with this perishable body made up of ice cream, pizza, bananas, you are not going to be perfect. The purpose of yogic training is to transcend the body, the chemical substance and realize that immortal state which you are.

THE VITAL SHEATH

Energy is subtle matter. Matter is energy on a dense gross level. The yogis speak about the prāṇamaya kośa, the invisible energy body. It consists of matter, though it is invisible to the naked eye. Even though we cannot see x-rays, that does not mean that they do not exist. A dog can hear a dog whistle, but we cannot. Because you can't hear it, it does not mean there is no sound. In the same way, because we are unable to see and detect the prāṇamaya kośa, that does not mean it doesn't exist.

Control of this prāṇamaya kośa, partially or fully, is important in all spiritual and psychic developments. In fact, we cannot exist without the prāṇamaya kośa; we are utilizing it in our day-to-day life. During dream, this prāṇamaya kośa is active, as well as during mesmeric trance or a real spiritual healing. A person may be extremely sick, and then the next day he or she is perfectly well, because this great powerful prāṇamaya kośa has been activated. When acupuncture doctors insert needles and pins, they are activating the prāṇamaya kośa, even though they may not know what it really is.

During prāṇayama, it is this kośa which is being activated. This current is called prāṇa. It is not oxygen. Do not confuse oxygen with prāṇa. Oxygen is a chemical gas. It can be carried through the blood stream. Prāṇa can be carried both in the astral system as well as the physical system. When it manifests through the physical system in the nervous system, then it is called a nerve current, for example in the spinal cord and the brain.

ĀSANA

THE HIGHER EFFECTS OF ĀSANAS

Āsana means posture.

The āsanas are divided into two categories: Cultural postures as well as meditative postures. The posture in which we are sitting is called meditative posture. The āsanas, where you move various joints into flexion, extension, hyper-extension, pronation, supination, elevation, depression, where we do various movements with the muscles to move the joints – these are called cultural postures. To get full control over the meditative posture, you must practice the cultural postures. According to Lord Śiva, there are 840,000 cultural postures. Out of these 84 are important, we know about 100 variations. Most of these postures and variations you can see in my *Complete Illustrated Book of Yoga*. While performing these cultural postures we are not only strengthening and stretching the muscles, but these āsanas also relate to the psychic system, which is called prāṇa.

Energy Blockages

When there is immobility between two vertebrae, several things happen:

- It affects the muscles and increases stress in the muscle.
- It affects the ligaments, which hold the joints together, thus decreasing local circulation.

- The nerves emanating from the spinal cord, are compressed by this immobility.
- Nerve irritation sets in, and this nerve irritation eventually will affect the mind itself.
- When there is again further nerve irritation and there is suppression of the nerve currents, the muscles or organs cannot function properly.

If you cut off a nerve from a muscle, what will happen? Though the muscle is healthy and alive, if you shut off the nerve current, it will die eventually, as the nerve current is not continuously flowing. In acupuncture theory, which is also the yogic theory, these nerve currents are either activated or shut off or short-circuited by applying metallic needles. The nerve currents are like electricity. Just like electricity is carried by wires, the nerve currents are carried by the nerves. These nerve currents are what the acupuncture therapist tries to stimulate. Suppose there is a pressure on a certain nerve, so the flow of the nerve current is limited to the liver, the kidneys, or the spleen. So, they put needles on specific points, called acupuncture points.

Reducing the Resistance

Take this example: Here is the microphone. From there my voice is being converted into electrical impulses, which go through the wire back into the tape recorder, and there it creates a kind of magnetic reaction in the tape. Suppose if I put a resistor between this microphone and the tape recorder, even though my voice is being activated, and the electrical impulses of my voice are now going through the microphone. The resistor will affect the flow of the electrical current, and eventually, when you replay the recording, the sound quality will not be good or even inaudible. So, what do you do? You take out the resistor and repeat the recording. Now the current flows freely.

That is what acupuncture is doing. When a needle is put on a nerve point, it is short-circuiting, reducing the resistance. Sometimes even an electrical stimulation is applied through the needle. The resistance is being reduced. Suppose the liver is not getting enough prāṇa, or nerve current, then by this stimulation the liver gets activated. You cannot all the time put needles all over your body, and sit or walk with needles, that would be very uncomfortable.

Stimulating the Flow of Prāṇa

So how to get the energy flow without any needles? How to reduce the resistance? That is one of the main purposes of āsanas. When you do a forward bend or a backward bend or a twist, 31 pairs of spinal nerves are affected. We are removing the pressure from these nerves. When there is less pressure, there is less resistance and prāṇa moves freely. At that time the muscles become very active, and the organs can function at their fullest capacity. The āsana system releases prāṇa into various organs. Otherwise, the light bulb will not shine, even though the bulb is in good condition. If I put a resistor in the cable, the bulb is the same, but the shining of the bulb depends on the amount of current flowing into the bulb.

In the same way, your physical and mental brilliance depends on the amount of prāṇa flowing into your physical system from your astral body. Anxieties, worries, tensions, mental afflictions, and poisons in your blood stream, all these increase the resistance, and the flow of prāṇa will be very little. At that time, though you are alive, you are just like a dim bulb. People say, "Hey, you look like a dead person." You are not dead, but people already say that you are dead. Sometimes even you yourself say, "I feel dead today." If you are dead, then how are you talking? What do you mean when you say, "I am dead"? If the energy would be coming from food, then you only would have to swallow some vitamins and minerals, proteins, and carbohydrates. And suddenly your body should be more alive, is it not? When you feel "dead", and you try to swallow all the vitamins, minerals proteins and carbohydrates, then your body will become even more dead, because absorbing these substances needs lots of energy. So, if it is not just the food that makes you shine, what then makes your face shine? What makes your eyes sparkle? Some people have tremendous personality. What does this mean? It is the strong flow of prāṇa from your astral system. For that you do not have to go to any beauty parlour. Your face will show. There is something shining within. And just like a shining bulb, you will see your face shine and your eyes will be sparkling. You will have a magnetic and pure aura.

That is what yogis have been speaking about for thousands of years: thought is not just an imaginary thing. It is a force, a power, like electricity or radiation. The pranic currents and the thoughts are very powerful in a yogi because the body can reduce the resistance. Therefore, a yogi can perform more action. Thus, the āsanas you are doing are not just physical exercise to move the joints, though joints are involved. You are also involving the thought currents, the pranic currents and allowing the prāṇa to move unrestricted. Thus, the higher aspect of āsanas is energetic, regulating the life energy.

PRĀṆA

PRĀṆA AND THOUGHT

When I speak to you and you speak to me, we do so using a limited frequency or wavelength. But when prophets like Jesus and Swami Sivananda speak, they have a tremendous prāṇa, a powerful energy that keeps resonating. These waves will go on reverberating continuously for several centuries.

For example, the *Rāmāyaṇa*, the story of Lord Rāmā, took place several thousand years ago. But that energy is still moving, and sages were able to tune to it in their meditation, connecting to these vibrations in the pineal gland area of their brain. The sage Vālmīki was able to visualize these events which happened in a previous age and then wrote down what he saw. Your thoughts become powerful only when there is tremendous prāṇa. Ordinary thoughts are like children playing with a walky-talky; the frequency carries only a few hundred yards.

It is the amount of prāṇa which defines your personality, your beauty, and how you are going to be attracted or be repulsed by another person. Prāṇa can manifest as powerful positive thoughts. When they unite, we call this marriage. Other thoughts may be very negative, there is no union. The other person is considered an enemy. We call this hate. Love and hate are both energized by prāṇa.

Thought is Energy

Once you start practicing prāṇāyāma and meditation regularly, your thoughts become very powerful because of the pranic current. Your thoughts will manifest. That is the law. No thought will go without manifestation. If you think "I want to become a millionaire", then you will become a millionaire within a few days depending upon how powerful your thoughts are. If the thoughts are not powerful, it may take thousands of years. But the thought is not wasted, it will materialize.

That you must understand and then only will you understand yoga. Thought is not just something vague. It is most powerful. What makes thoughts powerful is prāṇa. Prāṇa is personality; it is the beauty of a person or a flower; and it is the strength of a powerful politician. The prāṇa is still more powerful in prophets like Jesus or like our Master Sivananda. Their thoughts are still coming to you. I am interpreting them right now through my body and my mind. You all came not because of my power. It is his energy manifesting through me, and I am passing it on to you. Then you transfer it to your students. The more you practice prāṇāyāma, the more your personality will become stronger and powerful. You will then become a center of attraction.

Transmission of Prāṇa

If there is not enough prāṇa, your presence is like a dead body. There is very little prāṇa there, like in a drunkard. Who wants to go and see that person? You don't want to be near such persons because they discharge the prāṇa from you. When you visit a sick person, your prāṇa is taken out. A mother also passes on her prāṇa to her sick child. She puts her hands over the child's body and transfers the prāṇa. If you hit an iron post in the darkness what is the first thing you will do? You will hold the breath like in prāṇāyāma, and you transfer energy through your thoughts and your hands to the place where it hurts.

When the Pope blesses you, what is he doing? He raises his hands. You are then supposed to concentrate on your God in him and feel that his body is like an antenna which connects you to God. Outside this hall there is a painting where Jesus is putting his hands on a disciple, transferring prāṇa, giving blessings. So, whether it is Jesus or a Pope conferring blessings, or a priest is putting his hands on a sick person, or a mother placing her hands over the child, or a husband placing his hands on the feet of his wife: we are transmitting prāṇa and we transfer thoughts along with that. You can increase the prāṇa and recharge the solar plexus like a battery. That is the purpose of prāṇāyāma. It is not mere physical breathing. Thought and prāṇa go together. Your life is dependent on your thoughts. Success or failure depend on your thoughts. Depending on your prāṇa, thoughts become powerful.

AWAKENING THE ŚAKTI

We are in a remote area, away from the hustle and bustle of the world. Your purpose is to find Śānti, peace. Śānti, peace, God, ānanda, bliss is all one and the same. This requires lifting your energy level, which we do with the practice of prāṇāyāma.

Different types of energy are necessary for different purposes. A candle gives energy in the form of light and heat. There is electricity which also gives light and heat, that is also śakti or energy. Gravity is the energy which pulls everything towards the center of the earth. Muscular energy allows movement. There is also the energy of the mind, which allows the intellect to function, as well as the senses, the digestive system and the central nervous system. It also takes energy to simply sit quietly.

Sitting quietly needs more energy than working 10 hours outside with a shovel. To close your eyes, to sit quietly, and to keep the mind calm, needs a tremendous amount of energy. Just sitting quietly and bringing the mind inward requires a very different energy than going outside to some kind of entertainment. Bringing the mind inward needs a tremendous amount of energy.

Somehow, we have escaped this weekend to this remote area. The purpose is to find the method to control the turbulent mind and to make it calm. That is called lifting the energy level up. When the energy goes downward to the lower cakras, there is confusion, there are disturbances in the mind, which bring unhappiness, pain, dissatisfaction, and emotional conflict.

Focusing the Energy

To awaken the energy and raise the śakti or the energy level you need to gather the scattered rays of energy. When the energy is scattered like the rays of the sun, it becomes very sluggish and slow, and you are incapable of achieving anything. When the rays of the sun are pinpointed to a small area through a magnifying glass, they become very intense and can burn objects. On the level of the lower cakras, or plexuses, the energy is scattered, it is not one-pointed. Through prāṇāyāma, āsanas, and meditation, you can bring this one-pointed energy to the different cakras. The cakras magnify the energy. This is how the energy in the highest cakra becomes very intense and powerful. The awakening of the śakti from the lower to the higher cakras needs training and practice.

Even in the short time of this yoga weekend, you can increase your energy level. That is why we go away from the cities to mountains, forests, or other places where there is less distraction for the mind. You will see the difference after these two days. You will return with a new type of peace, strength, and awareness.

This experience is subjective, nobody can give it to you. You must experience it yourself. I can only talk about the sweetness of honey. But unless and until you taste the honey you will never know what honey means. During this weekend we are going to explain the technique of tasting this honey, which you must taste by yourself. The first and foremost thing is to use the right time, which is early in the morning. This time is called brahmamuhurta. It is the best time to uplift your energy level. The rays of the rising sun have a definite effect on your psychic system. The sun radiates various types of energy in the form of colors. These colors are energies. We call these visible colors violet, indigo, blue, green, yellow, orange, and red. But they are not actually colors, they are nothing but waves. Violet is the highest frequency. Red, on the other end of the spectrum, is the lowest frequency. In between, lie various frequencies which we call yellow, orange, etcetera.

We all have heard about laser. Laser uses only one frequency. It can penetrate through solid objects. It can break molecules by heating them. Laser is now being uses to play sound recordings. Laser is even being used for minute surgery of the eyes. Similarly, the kuṇḍalinī śakti is an energy far beyond our understanding at present. We must awaken this śakti, and each cakra represents a particular wavelength. Just like each of the seven visible colors has a particular wavelength, so also the seven cakras. We are increasing our energy level from the lower to a higher wavelength as we go upward.

That is the purpose of chanting *Om Namo Nārāyanāya, Hare Rāma,* of prāṇāyāma and āsanas. Different methods need to be used to lift the energy level up. Besides the physical body, we have a subtle, astral, or psychic body which includes the intellectual sheath. And we have the causal body or blissful sheath. All these bodies must be tuned to the adequate wavelength. When all these wavelengths together are tuned to a very proper tone, then there will be peace, śānti. That is called meditation.

Śiva and Śakti

In yogic literature, Śakti has different meanings. It literally means power. Generally, Śakti is defined as feminine, not masculine. The masculine has no power, only the feminine. In Indian theology, Śiva is masculine, and his creative feminine power is Śakti. It manifests in various names and forms like Durga, Parvati, Saraswati, Lakshmi, Kali, etc. Śiva and Śakti are always one. They are not two. One cannot exist without the other. Śiva has got no power without Śakti. Śiva is incapable of performing anything without Śakti. But Śakti cannot exist without the substratum of Śiva. So, from the highest point of view, they are not two, they are one.

Sometimes you can see a spider alone without a web. It has no home. It is independent. It wanders from one place to another. At that time the web is inside of the spider. When it decides to make a home, it brings a huge web out of its own mouth. It can move anywhere in the web, whereas any fly that comes into the web will get stuck. But the spider is not caught in its own web.

This example is to illustrate Śiva and Śakti. Śiva and Śakti are one, and then there is separation. That is when the spider creates its web. Now there appear to be two, the spider and its web. After some time, the spider will withdraw the web back into its own body. The web becomes again one with the spider. When Śakti comes out of Śiva, it is called evolution or creation. When she becomes again one with Śiva, it is called dissolution or pralāya. But Śiva always remains same. How much web comes out of the spider's body, doesn't diminish the size of its body.

Śiva is inactive. He only watches. It is Śakti which activates all functions. It is functioning even now. Look at all those beautiful spring flowers. In the winter, everything was lying buried under the snow. When Spring comes, we see beautiful tulips, the trees are budding with flowers, Śakti is exploding. Śakti functions in different ways. In the nature she becomes flowers, trees, shrubs, and fruits. Then she manifests as higher evolved beings, like animals. According to the yogic scriptures, there are 840,000 species. It is the Śakti which evolved from one species to another.

Evolution According to Yoga Philosophy

We are not talking about Darwin's theory here. That is entirely opposite to the yogic system. It is not that a monkey will change one day into a human being. If that would be so, when did the monkey change into a human being, on which date? Was it on January 1st in 5000 BC? Suddenly some monkeys started walking on two legs and they became your forefathers? If that would be so, why did no monkeys before or after that date start to walk on two feet? Have you ever seen any monkey change into a human being?

Swami Sivananda has written a humorous story about the question whether monkeys have become humans: A dozen monkeys sat on a mango tree and discussed certain things. One monkey said: "Now listen to me. People say that man descended from us. No monkey ever divorced his wife. No monkey ever starved his children. No monkey abandoned his children and took sanyāsa (monkhood). No monkey smokes, gambles, drinks, and dances in a club. No monkey suffers from syphilis and takes medical injections. No monkey marries a fourth wife at 80. No monkey takes another monkey's life with a gun or knife or an atom bomb. It is quite sure that humankind did not descend from us. Darwin is incorrect in his statement."

According to the yogic theory, you must evolve through 840,000 stages. Throughout this evolution the soul remains the same. Suppose a spider dies today, then its soul will now take a slightly higher form in the scale of evolution. The spider will take birth as a small mosquito. Now it can fly around and put injections into you. When the mosquito dies, it will reach the next stage, maybe a beautiful parrot. Then from a parrot it becomes a big eagle. When it dies as an eagle, it may then become an amphibian, like a tortoise. At one point it is born as an elephant with a more evolved brain, until finally it is born as a human being after passing step by step through 840,000 wombs.

It is not the soul which is evolving but the vehicle which changes according to the evolution. During the first few thousand human lives you were no better than animals. What do animals want? They want only four things: āhāra or food, nidrā or sleep, bhaya or fear so they know how to survive through the fight or flight mechanism, and then maithunaṁ or procreation. These are the only four things which animals want. Still now many human beings only want these four.

Vibratory Levels of Śakti

When the Śakti came out of Śiva, this separation became the ājñā cakra. Then further separation took place from ājñā to viśuddha cakra, the ethereal centre. From there to the heart centre or anāhata cakra, which is the centre of the gases or vāyu, air. From there it became the maṇipūra cakra, the seat of fire at the navel centre. Then on to the sex centre or svādhiṣṭhāna cakra, which is the element water. Finally, it became the last centre of the spinal column, which is called mūlādhāra, or earth centre. Once it reached this very last state, the Śakti cannot go any further down. This last element is the final state.

Each of the elements is a particular wavelength. The microphone in my hand is a piece of metal, solid matter, or earth element. But a scientist will tell you that it is nothing but electrons, protons, and neutrons, it is made of waves. Yogis knew thousands of years ago that there are only waves, no solid matter. When the Śakti appears as liquid, this is only our perception. Water consists of hydrogen and oxygen. In this state it can quench your thirst. If you bring hydrogen near the fire it will explode. If you bring oxygen near the fire, the fire becomes big. When you mix the two together, it becomes water. If you put water near the fire, it will put out the fire.

Śakti changes into different patterns. Whether water is in a solid state as ice, or liquid as water, or when it becomes steam, it is still H_2O. Only its property changed. For our perception it is called solid, liquid or gas but not from the Śakti's point of view. Depending on the wavelength we call it ether, or ākāśa in Sanskrit. In the next wavelength she is gas. When gases start to whirl around, she becomes fire like the Sun. Then the Śakti further solidifies and becomes liquid like lava, in the core of our planet earth. When lava comes out of the volcano, it solidifies and becomes rock. Solid, liquid, gas etc. is only for our senses. Only the wavelengths change. The grossest wavelength of Śakti is the earth principle.

Awakening of Consciousness

When the kuṇḍalinī śakti is resting or sleeping, she is still active, but her wavelength is very low. It corresponds to the thousands of previous lives where we incarnate in human bodies but behave just like animals: eating, sleeping, procreating, and following the survival instinct. Then in one life, the Śakti's wavelength changes, it is no more dormant, the kuṇḍalinī awakens. The first sign of that awakened consciousness is that hot dogs, hamburgers, caviar, and champagne appear to be poison. A club with topless, bottomless, and brainless dancers becomes painful to see.

Why did you to this place? There is nothing to see here except some pictures of Kṛṣṇa, flowers, and candles. None of these will give you any excitement.

Two years ago, after a late-night lecture in Paris, someone was driving me through that particular street where I saw girls with shorts, without socks or anything. I am not talking here in a bad way. They were standing there in the cold hardly dressed. To make a living they stand in the cold until 2 or 3 o'clock in the morning to find a customer.

If you ask someone to come and meditate here at 2 o'clock in the morning, the person will complain that it is too cold here.

I was pitying these girls who were standing there in the cold just to make a living, by pleasing some men for money. With the money they make they cannot escape their situation. There are men behind who control them and who take most of the money. These men are sitting comfortably in the warm house while these girls are standing outside in the cold. Just see the karma of these people. You cannot ask them to please come so we can teach them that happiness is within you, have them repeat *Om Namo Nārāyanāya,* and teach them standing on the head early in the morning.

Here it is different. You are trying to get out of those structures of matter. The fact that you come and sit here for this weekend in a simple place, away from the comforts and conveniences of your home – it is the first sign that the kuṇḍalinī is awakening. If this would not be so, it would not be possible for you get up at 5.30am in the morning and meditate here without breakfast or coffee, without champagne or a party in the evening. What are you going to do this evening? Chant OM. You tell your friends I went for an awakening holiday. What did you do? I woke up at 5.30am, washed myself with cold water and chanted OM. Then they give us some carrots or rabbit food and ask us to inhale and exhale. For that you travelled 200 miles? You are really crazy!

But when the Śakti awakens, those things of which once you thought as real, they become unreal and painful. This happens of course in different degrees because your evolution still goes on. But when the Śakti is vibrating at a high level, when she goes to the higher cakras, then the vibratory level goes up. From mūlādhāra to swadisthana, maṇipūra, anāhata, viśuddha, ājñā and then to sahasrāra. That is called union. That return of the Śakti, when she again unites with Śiva, takes many billions of years. But you can hasten this process by practicing āsana, prāṇāyāma, japa, meditation, satsaṅg etc. That is the theory.

How Prāṇa Manifests

Śakti manifests now in all living beings as prāṇa śakti. On this level, she is not called kuṇḍalinī śakti, but prāṇa śakti. We also call it electricity. In Sanskrit, electricity is called viddhu śakti, or the manifestation of Śakti in all living things. We cannot describe it in English or any other language, but the closest is the term vitality or vital energy.

For example, look at this nice flower, is it not beautiful? You want to touch and smell it. That is called prāṇa śakti. We are not touching physical matter which is nothing but the earth. A few days ago, the flower was still underground and now it has become a beautiful flower composed of earth, water and minerals. If you bring this flower to your loved one, your wife or your husband, what exactly does it represent? My love is just like this blooming flower. You don't have to talk when you give the flower, you don't have to even say I love you honey, you just give that flower to a loved one. Now imagine that the husband brought a bunch of plastic flowers, what will the wife do? She will hit him with these flowers. The reason is that in the plastic flower, there is no prāṇa. The prāṇa is what makes it beautiful.

I observed a small incident during a yoga symposium in another ashram in California. There was a septic area and flies started breeding there. We were given some kind of fly trap: a big bottle with a black hood. The flies can go inside through a small hole. Inside they smell a commercial kind of liquid, which smells like dead rats. But for the flies it smells like Chanel 5 or Chanel 6 perfume. They come from everywhere trying to enjoy this smell. But after enjoying it they cannot get out, they are trapped. From your point of view, it smells horrible, but from the flies' point of view it is like the best French perfume. When Śakti vibrates in a particular wavelength, other creatures may get attracted to it. We can only get attracted to one particular wavelength. In the plastic flower there is very little wavelength or prāṇa. A live flower and a plastic flower are not the same.

That's why two people meet and without much introduction they fall in love. It is because the wavelength, the prāṇa and the thought are similar. Everybody has prāṇa, but in some people, it is depleted, due to the consumption of alcohol, drugs, tobacco, meat, garlic etc. which all change the vibration of the pranic level. The energy becomes rajasic and tamasic, whereas in a place like this, the chanting, the sattvic, pure vegetarian food lift the vibratory level.

Look at the prāṇa in the picture of Gurudev Sivananda's face. I lived with him for several years. When you come near him, you don't want to leave his presence. It is not even necessary to talk to him, you just want to stay near him. It is due to the prāṇa. We all have prāṇa, but it is at a low level. Here, in this monastery, as soon as I arrived, I was in meditation for several hours. It comes automatically because you can feel the vibration.

When I went on pilgrimage in India, the vibration was so pure. There were wild insects, wild elephants. I could stay in those jungles forever, watching the birds and animals, the beautiful streams and waterfalls. It all lifts up your mind. Compared to that, all the chandeliers in a five-star hotel are just like plastic flowers. It is completely different from the natural surroundings where sages meditate.

We come to this retreat to increase the prāṇa.

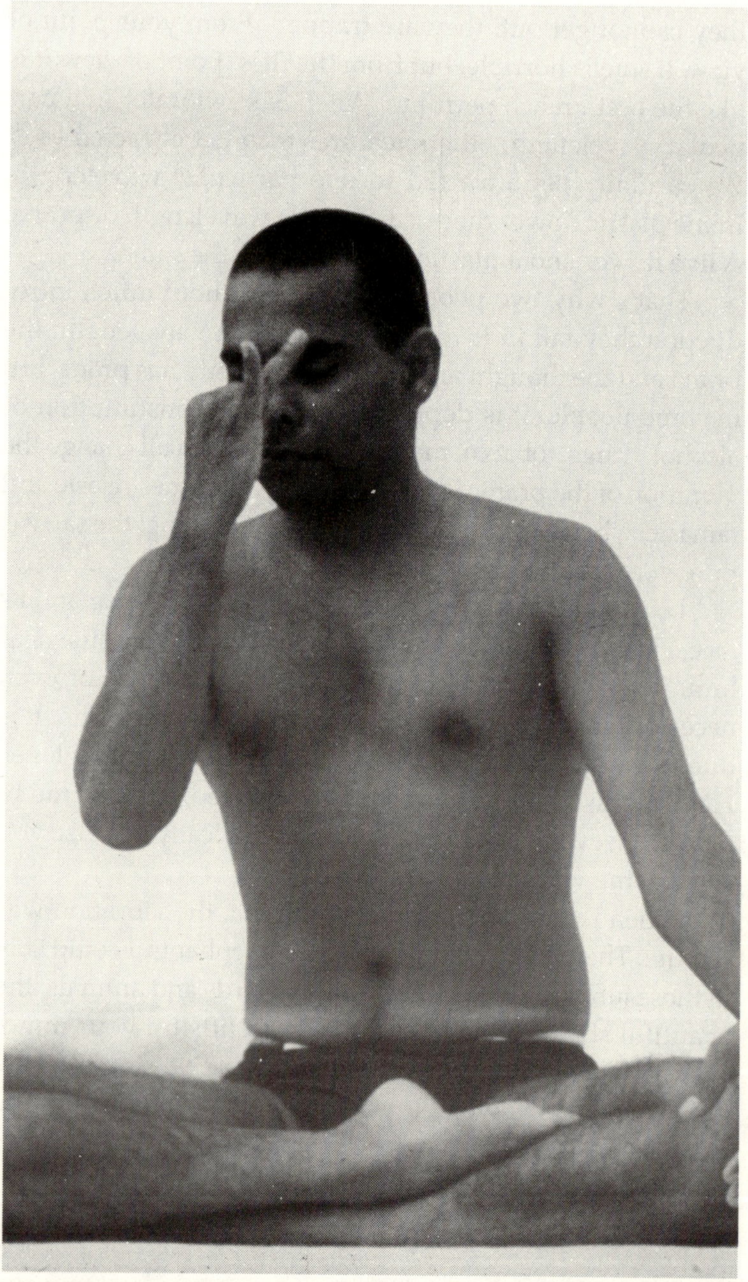

PRĀṆĀYĀMA

THREE LEVELS OF BREATH CONTROL

The first level of breath control is physical breathing: you learn how to use the respiratory muscles such as the diaphragm and the intercostal muscles. It is breathing in a smooth rhythm, according to the oxygen needs of the body. The second level of breath control is the vital or psychic breathing: you learn to unite the subtle energies ha and ṭha. Ha is the sun. Ṭha is the moon. These are synonyms of yin and yang or prāṇa and apāna. The union of both is haṭha. Haṭha yoga is not just standing on the head, as many people think. When you can unite these two energies, the kuṇḍalinī is awakened and goes to the heart cakra. From there it reaches the higher centers.

The third level of breath control is called mental breathing. It is with this level that you will obtain the full benefit of prāṇāyāma. If your breath is very irregular, it reflects in the way you speak, and the state of your mind. When the mind is disturbed, breathing is irregular.

How the Mind Influences the Breath

How much your lungs are expanding and contracting and in which rhythm, depends on the nature of your thoughts and your moods. There are seven basic emotions which affect our mood: lust, anger, greed, hatred, jealousy, envy, and fear. Not only when one is angry, but under the influence of any of these seven emotions, there will be major changes to the movement of the prāṇa through the 72,000 nāḍis. If any of these emotions is out of control, it can shatter your physical nervous system. This disturbance will then create a violent reaction in your endocrine system, in your thyroid, pituitary and pineal gland, as well as many other glands. Especially fear can destroy our equilibrium. But even a so-called happy mood can create an imbalance, when there is complete exhilaration due to some unexpected happy event. It can create a similar imbalance in the nervous and the endocrine system.

Here is a simple story: once there was an elderly poor couple. Both were cardiac patients with high blood pressure. They used to play in the state lottery. One day they won a million dollars. The lottery administrator was worried that they could have a heart attack if this news would be conveyed by telephone to them. So, she asked the local priest to personally go and inform them about the news in a diplomatic way. The couple was happy to have the visit of their priest. After spending some time with ordinary talk, the priest asked them: What would you do if you won one million dollars in the lottery?" The couple replied: "we would give half the money to your church!" – The priest dropped dead of a heart attack!

This is not just a story. People jump in joy when they make a large profit on the stock market. When the stock market goes up, their blood pressure also goes up. But when the stock market crashes, some people literally jump out of the window and commit suicide. Our emotions are constantly swinging like a pendulum between joy and sorrow, love and hate, good and bad. The pendulum is rarely in the center. This is the cause of many major diseases. Through meditation and yoga, you can learn to keep the pendulum in the center. It is very difficult to change mental habits. But when you do prāṇāyāma with proper concentration, you can find balance and hold the pendulum in the center. When your breath slows down, your impulses will also slow down.

Where the Mind Goes, the Prāṇa Goes

It is not merely a mechanical breath control. When you practice prāṇāyāma, you focus the mind on a particular cakra. Wherever you focus, there the prāṇa will go. Where the mind goes, the prāṇa goes. Through breath control and focusing on the higher cakras up to the third eye between the eyebrows, you can move the prāṇa. This can protect your nervous system from the effects of stress.

Without this balance and control of the prāṇa, both your nervous system and your endocrine system are at risk. Prāṇāyāma only works if you also practice āsanas. Through the āsanas, the stressful energy which accumulates in the muscles due to the imbalance of the nervous system, is released and expanded. This needs to be combined with proper diet and meditation. Only then can you keep the pendulum of your life in the center. When you hold the breath in prāṇāyāma you can feel the united prāṇa and apāna moving upward. At that time the mind will be very peaceful, free from both exhilaration and depression.

THE NATURE OF PRĀṆĀYĀMA

I will speak to you about an aspect of your body which you cannot see. We use it every minute, every second. Without this vehicle, you will not be able to function with your physical body. The physical body itself cannot function until some other force makes it work. It is like the planet earth. It is not moving by itself. There is an energy behind it, an invisible element which makes the planet move.

There are two types of energy, one is visible, and another is invisible. Which energy is more powerful, the visible or the invisible? It is the invisible. There are some giant trees, visible and broad, with solid roots in the ground. But then they are overthrown by the invisible wind. This is an easy concept. Another example is steam. You cannot see it, but it makes the engine move. Still more subtle than the wind is electricity. This invisible electricity can move huge weights and can travel at the speed of light. All this is possible due to this invisible force.

The Power of Thought

Beyond the electrical force, there is one more force which is still more powerful. That is the power of thought. Thought does not manifest in the physical brain. The physical brain is simply an accumulation of cells. It is the media through which the mind communicates with the physical world. All physical sense perception is directed to the mind through the brain. Mind and thought are the most powerful force. The mind and thoughts are the same, just like the waves and the ocean are one and the same. The waves are not different from the ocean.

What is the mind? Where are thoughts? What is the relation between prāṇa and the thoughts? Rāja yoga teaches "*yoga's-citta-vṛtti-nirodhaḥ*" – "yoga is controlling or subjugating the mental modifications." Patanjali explains that there are five types of thought waves in the mind. Some are pleasant, others are not pleasant. Looking at the light of a candle is very pleasant. But when you touch it, it becomes painful.

Thought is the greatest force. To manifest the thought, energy is necessary. Just like a candle cannot burn without oxygen, so also thought cannot exist without prāṇa. Without oxygen the candle is just a piece of matter, it cannot give light and heat. It is a dormant energy. Only when combined with oxygen it will give light and heat. The mind is like a candle. By itself, it cannot do anything. But when prāṇa acts on the mind, suddenly it becomes powerful.

The mind in a yogi is more powerful than in ordinary people, because his or her mind is charged with prāṇa. Prāṇa is directed like a single beam. It is like focusing the sunrays through a lens and pinpointing them. These pinpointed rays burn objects. In the same way when the mind is concentrated through thought and prāṇa, and is focused in one area, it becomes powerful. That is called concentration and meditation. Meditation and concentration are one and the same. Concentration is the beginning stage, the first stage of meditation. Meditation is the perfection of concentration.

When you try to focus the thoughts in any one area, it moves away. That is the natural tendency of the mind. If you know how to focus the mind in one area and keep it there, then there is nothing for you to look for. All riddhis (good fortune) and siddhis (powers) will come at your feet. In fact, there is nothing external to you. All the powers, all that is happening, is not external to you. There is nothing to be achieved through an external source. It is all within you. Why can you not obtain it at this moment? Because of the scattered rays of the mind.

Haṭha Yoga and Rāja Yoga are One

Haṭha yoga and rāja yoga are one and the same. There is no difference. Haṭha yoga explains prāṇa in more detail. Rāja yoga starts directly with thought. In the ancient days, rāja yoga was taught, because everyone knew about āsanas and prāṇāyāma. Already as a child, they were taught prāṇāyāma in detail. It was part of their daily life. In the gurukula system, the student went and stayed with the teacher for 12 to 14 years. By the time he finished his studies, he knew all the prāṇāyāmas, bandhas, mudras etc. There was no problem for him to learn thought control. Only later, people were not aware anymore of these basic aspects of rāja yoga. So, more attention had to be given to āsanas and prāṇāyāma.

Haṭha yoga is not just āsanas and prāṇāyāma, haṭha yoga is rāja yoga in a scientific and detailed study. All the practical techniques in rāja yoga point to haṭha yoga. Haṭha yoga is the practical aspect of rāja yoga, and rāja yoga is the creative aspect of haṭha yoga. They are like the obverse and reverse of the same coin. In the haṭha yoga system, to control the mind, you must learn to control the prāṇa. Because the waves in the lake are caused by the wind. If there is no wind, there will be no waves and the mind will be very calm. If you want to keep the mind calm, you must know how to control the prāṇa. To control the prāṇa, you must know how to control the physical breath.

Breath, Prāṇa and Mind

The relation between the physical breath, the prāṇa and the mind is like this: when you look at the trees and there is no motion in the leaves, it means that the air is not moving, that there is no wind. You cannot see the air. But by looking at the leaves you know that the air is not in motion. When the leaves flutter, you know that this is caused by the wind. You can conclude that the air is moving.

Similarly, when there is physical breathing, there is

motion. That physical motion is like the fluttering of the leaves. In the same way when a person is breathing there is prāṇa. The prāṇa strikes in the form of nerve currents. These nerve currents are initiated in the brain and from there they are continuously moving in form of impulses to the diaphragm. When you want to suspend the prāṇa, you must suspend the physical breath. You are suspending the impulses coming to your respiratory center in the brain and that suspends the impulses to the diaphragm.

It can be compared to a nerve impulse which travels to a skeletal muscle. The impulses come from my brain and make my muscle contract. As a result, the joint flexes. Then impulses come to the opposite muscles and the joint extends. If I touch that nerve which reaches the muscle, it will not make a difference. I will not be able to flex or extend the joint, because there is no nerve impulse generated in the brain.

The same kind of impulse is reaching your respiratory center in the brain continuously, day and night, even when you sleep. Even when you are at rest, still the impulses are coming, and you are breathing very slowly. Suddenly the mind becomes agitated. The impulses coming from the brain are becoming deeper and irregular. Have you seen a person upset and angry? Do you remember how is your breathing when you are upset and angry? The impulses are like a strong wind. The breath and the mind are agitated. The impulses coming from the brain are also agitated. They reach the intercostal muscles and make your breathing move violently in the wrong direction. (i.e. the abdomen contracts during inhalation) In the contrary when your mind is calm, the impulses coming from the brain are very gentle. (i.e. the abdomen expands during inhalation). When you are meditating, it is very gentle.

Let us do a small test now. Close your eyes. I'm going to

tap like that. Please count how many times I am tapping. Concentrate very well and try to find out how many times I am tapping. – Now tell me, what happened to your breathing? It stopped or it became very slow. I asked you to concentrate on the sound. I did not ask you to concentrate on your breath or to control the breath. As you focused your thoughts on the sound to count it, you had to breathe very rhythmically. Otherwise, you were not able to control your thoughts and concentrate. To focus the thoughts, you must have control over the prāṇa.

When you want to lift a heavy object, you hold your breath. All the weightlifters hold their breath. It is not just the physical holding of the breath, there is a psychology behind it. They lift an enormous amount of weight compared to the size of their muscle. How do they do that? They are not only training their muscles. They prepare their mind. They learn breath control, concentration, and the psychological affirmation "I am going to lift this weight." The psychological preparation and the mental affirmations are very important. Without it, no matter how well the muscles are developed, they cannot lift that weight. First, they must keep their minds focused and make their thoughts strong. They must concentrate on the thought "I can lift it, I'm going to lift it, nothing can stop me." Only with that psychological preparation their muscles will obey. They cannot lift the same weight when the mind is upset.

Prana and Astral Body

This is what the yogis are saying since thousands of years: your physical body cannot function without prāṇa and thought. If you can control these, you are free. Thought and prāṇa are not coming from the brain. The physical brain itself is activated by another level which is called the mind. The mind is not in the physical body, it is in our inner body, the astral body. The astral body contains all your ten senses: the five senses of knowledge which are seeing (eyes), hearing (ears), smelling (nose), tasting (tongue) and touch (skin); and the five senses of action: hands (giving and taking), feet (moving), mouth (speech), organs of evacuation and the genital organs (reproduction).

These senses are not in the physical body. Even if someone loses a physical hand through amputation and the wound has healed, the person can still feel pain in their hand. It is called phantom pain. But it is not phantom pain. The astral hand is still there. Every physical body has a counter body, the astral body. During the Yoga Teachers' Training Course, you learn the detailed functions of the astral body step by step. The 10 senses are not in the physical body, they are in the astral body. The prāṇa, the vital energy is not in the physical body either, it is in the astral body. Prāṇa is divided into 5 categories: prāṇa (respiration), apāna (elimination and reproduction), samāna (digestion), udāna (swallowing), and vyāna (blood circulation). Just like electricity has a positive and a negative pole, so also prāṇa is divided into main currents. A magnet can convert electricity into magnetism, and magnetism into electricity. In the same way, prāṇa and thought go together. Prāṇa can be converted into thought and thought can be converted into prāṇa. They are all interrelated. Besides the five prāṇas and the ten senses, the astral body also contains the four mental functions or aspects of the mind: thinking/doubting, intellect, ego, and subconscious. All these make the 19 elements of the astral body.

The physical body is its counter form, the gross manifestation of the astral body. You have a physical body because of the astral body. The existence and nature of the physical body is the exact picture of the astral body. It is not the other way around: it is not because we have a physical body that we have an astral body. It is due to the condition of the astral body that we have certain conditions in the physical body.

Energy Patterns in the Physical Body

Even the number of days of your life are shown through your astral body in the form of the lines of your palms. The lines in your palm reflect these energy patterns. Sometimes the energy pattern of your lifeline is broken. You can see it in my hands. At the age of 48-49 approximatively, my lifeline ended in both hands. I died last November in a hospital in Spain. I came back to life, I was resuscitated. Death itself is not painful, it is very beautiful. I did not want to come back. Who wants to come back? It is more peaceful there. It is like a deep meditation, nothing uncertain at all.

The life pattern can be seen in the palm, it looks like it is ending. We do not see a complete life pattern in anybody's palm. The energy pattern continues to form it. Everything is an energy pattern. It also shows in the pattern of the hand. My hand has a square form. It is a practical hand, not an artistic hand. An artistic hand would be long. The fingers would be long. I cannot draw with my hand. My hand is not for any drawing purpose. If I draw a mouse, it looks like a mosquito. It won't look like a mouse. It is a practical hand. Anything I imagine, I put it into practice, into practical life. That is my nature. All the lines on the palm correspond to energy patterns. Headline, heartline, lifeline, and you can see the mystical cross in the center of both hands.

Your hand and your face are also energy patterns. The way we look, how long the forehead is, the neck and the eyebrows, and how full the eyebrows are, the shape of the nose, even the pattern of how the hair falls – these are all energy patterns. The energy in the astral body moves in a specific pattern. No matter what I do, that curl will always be there, because the energy flows in one direction. This is not just physical; it is all astral.

Prana and Nadis

Air is composed of different gases such as oxygen, carbon dioxide and nitrogen, as well as many other gases. Similarly, prāṇa performs different functions. Prāṇa is not oxygen. Just like oxygen is tied to the bloodstream, so the prāṇa is tied to the nāḍis or the nervous system.

There are 72,000 astral nerves called nāḍis. And every astral nerve has a physical nerve as a counter part in the physical body. There are 3 major nāḍis, which are iḍā, piṅgala and suṣumṇa. Generally, the suṣumṇa, the central nāḍi is blocked. It opens very seldom, unless one is a very evolved soul. The energy mostly flows through the other 71,999 nāḍis. Suṣumṇa nāḍi is the one nāḍi which is completely blocked. Until you open that nāḍi, there is no peace, no happiness. To open this nāḍi is the aim. Prāṇāyāma is not made for oxygen's sake. Its purpose is to open that one energy channel.

The iḍā and piṅgala nāḍis correspond to the motor and sensory nerves in the physical body. One set of nerves carries impulses from the brain to the body; these nerves are called motor nerves. The sensory impulses are carrying impulses from the body to the brain. When you see an object, it is sensory, it comes from the senses. The motor and the sensory nerves are also called efferent and afferent. In Sanskrit, in yogic terminology, they are called iḍā and piṅgala nerve currents. Ordinarily it is the iḍā and the piṅgala, the sensory and motor impulses which are functioning. Advanced yogis shut off these impulses and direct the energy to the suṣumṇa. At that time, you are dead to the world. There is no sensory perception of the external world for you. Instead, there is transcendental experience. That experience is not coming from contact with the senses. It comes directly from within your own Self because the mind is still. When the prāṇa goes into the suṣumṇa, the mind cannot function.

When the prāṇa only goes to iḍā and piṅgala, then the mind is agitated. When the prāṇa goes to the suṣumṇa, the mind is still. This is the philosophy behind haṭha yoga. Haṭha yoga is a complete and scientific way of controlling the mind. For more details, please read the *Complete Illustrated Book of Yoga.*

Primary and Secondary Vital Impulse

The plants also breathe, but not for oxygen's sake. The plants inhale carbon dioxide and exhale oxygen. Just like we inhale oxygen and exhale carbon dioxide. So, there is balance. Some yogis live buried underground without oxygen for 7 - 8 days. Some people get caught in an avalanche and are completely buried under the snow. For several hours there is no air and their heartbeat and the brain waves stop. But then the rescue team comes and searches with long rods, with a light attached. Every two feet they push the rod into the snow. When they find and dig up the person, the body is completely frozen. There was no oxygen and therefore no heartbeat and brain waves, and still the person can survive. According to the yogic theory oxygen is only for the physical movement, just like fire needs oxygen to burn. When you can lower the metabolic activity to a very low rate you do not need that much oxygen. That's why some yogis can stay underground in a very small box for 7 days. That amount of air is quite sufficient for the body to survive. It is like artificial hibernation. The metabolic functions are slowed down. There is nothing extraordinary, nothing unscientific about it.

The impulse which comes from the brain to the diaphragm and the intercostal muscles is called prāṇa. It is the primary impulse of all living creatures. It makes us breathe in order to live.

When someone pushes your head under the water, the first thought you have is to breathe. Are there any other thoughts at that time? Do you think of your wife or husband at that time, or of a pizza or a cigarette? At that time there is only one thought: Oh Lord, let me have my breath. That primary impulse comes in the form of the motion of the lungs. It corresponds to the most powerful thought in all living creatures, from an amoeba to a human being. Plants and everything that lives, all want to breathe.

After the primary impulse of breathing, there is the secondary impulse. This is the thought of procreation. Sex is the secondary impulse. Just like the impulse coming from the brain is continuously reaching the diaphragm and the intercostal muscles, so also the impulse from the lower cakras comes continuously to the sexual organs.

Just like you are sometimes aware of your breathing, and sometimes you are not aware of it, but still you are breathing, even when you sleep. In the same way, sexual impulses are produced even in dream and in deep sleep. Sometimes you are aware of it, sometimes you are not aware of it. When you are aware of it, it is called passion. It can become uncontrollable just like your breath becomes uncontrollable and irregular when anger comes. So also, passion can become uncontrollable and violent. At that time a man will commit many actions against his higher nature.

The secondary impulse is called apāna. This energy moves to the sexual organs and leads to sexual experience. The same energy is also the cause for elimination of urine and feces, and even the delivery of a child. This energy is always pushed outside your body, away from your body. It is called apāna in Sanskrit.

Prāṇa is the primary impulse, its function is motion of your lungs. Apāna leads to the sexual act which keeps the world moving. Otherwise, there would be no world. If you don't breathe there is no world. If there is no sexual act there is no reproduction in the world, everything comes to a collapse. So māyā, the world, wants to keep these two forces alive.

The Nature of the Sexual Impulse

But spiritual people do not want to use this energy. They know how to sublimate this energy upwards to the higher centers. Though the energy naturally flows to the lower sexual centers, you can also sublimate it to the higher centers. Then you will get supra-sensual experience. It is a thousand times higher; a beautiful dimension.

The experience that you get from the senses in the sexual experience is so crude, so finite, and it also completely depletes your energy within a few minutes. It takes several hours to replenish the energy you spend in sensual and sexual experience. In a fraction of a second most of the energy is short-circuited. The battery is drained completely. It takes many hours to recharge it again. A person who indulges continuously in sexual experience, loses the vital energy. The body will lose strength and become like a depleted battery. That's why a certain amount of control over sexual energy is an essential part of spiritual life. It's not that a sexual act is a sin or a bad thing. We are not talking in that sense at all.

Each body has only a certain amount of prāṇa in a lifetime which can be used. This is like a battery which has a certain lifetime before it must be recharged. If you are using the battery in your car, you can put the lights on, the heat and the tape recorder and all other appliances. If the engine is not running and recharging the battery how long will the battery last? Soon it will be finished, depleted. But if you use only one appliance like the radio, then the battery life will last longer than if you run all the appliances at once.

There is a lot of energy needed for all sensual and sexual experiences. Within a short time your body which is supposed to live in good health for 100 years is depleted.

Some people are alive, but they look like a dead person. There is no energy there, they look like a dead battery. All the psychic energy is continuously depleted through sexual experience. It is like milking a cow. You can only milk a cow in the morning and in the evening. If you try to milk a cow for 24 hours, you will only get blood. Similarly, you cannot milk this body beyond a certain limit no matter how much you try. That is why celibacy is needed, not complete 100% which is not possible for many people. But a certain amount of control of the sexual energy is part of prāṇāyāma. Then only the prāṇāyāma will be very successful. That is why I am giving you this explanation.

Practice of Breathing Exercises

Prāṇāyāma is not just merely controlling the physical breath. It is controlling the impulse to breathe. This primary impulse is called prāṇa. And then you control the secondary impulse called apāna. When you combine these two forces, prāṇa and apāna it is called prāṇāyāma, it is called haṭha yoga. At that time the energy will go into the suṣumṇa. Then you will get psychic experience and the prāṇa will start moving into the various higher centers.

This is the simplest explanation about prāṇāyāma which I can give you in this short time. Again, to remind you, read the *Complete Illustrated Book of Yoga* for more information. When you learn prāṇāyāma, first you learn the actual breathing exercises. You cannot do prāṇāyāma in the beginning, because for that you must have the control of both prāṇa and apāna. But you can learn the art of controlling the breath, and that is the purpose of teaching the breathing exercises.

MIND

THE MIND AND THE SENSES

Today is Monday, is it not? Yesterday was ... Sunday. So, what is the difference between Sunday and Monday? ... One day closer to death. But you are not one day closer to death, you are one day closer to immortality. While many people are wasting their time, you are doing something to help yourselves attain the immortal state or moksha, to attain the realization of the Self through meditation.

To reach that inner silence, we need to purify the mind. The mind is drawn towards the objects of the five senses. Eyes, ears, nose, tongue, and skin are the five sense organs of knowledge through which sense perception occurs. Each of these senses pulls the mind into its direction, and none of them can function without the help of the mind. This is the first point to remember: the mind by itself cannot have perception. It needs to attach itself to particular sense organs like the eyes or the ears.

One Sensory Impression at a Time

The second point is that the mind can only be associated with one sense at a time. If you are seeing, you cannot hear. It only appears that you are hearing and seeing a person at the same time. If you are hearing, you are not seeing and if you are seeing, you are not hearing. The analogy for this is

5 soft rose petals which are placed one on top of the other. Now a needle is piercing through the five rose petals. How long does it take the needle to penetrate the petals? It appears as if it happens all at once. But the needle pierces the five petals only one at a time. It doesn't matter how fast and with how much pressure the needle moves. Even if the needle would move at the speed of light, it would still only penetrate one petal at a time.

This also applies to the mind. The mind cannot hear, see, taste, touch, and smell at the same time. But it moves with lightning speed from sight to sound, from sound to taste, from taste to touch. The mind is continuously revolving from one sensory source to the next. It is due to this lightning speed that it appears as if you can see, hear, taste, smell, and touch at the same time. When you are reading attentively some novel or a newspaper, and someone calls your name to remind you that it is time for dinner: Do you hear the words? The call for dinner is there, but your mind is concentrating on reading. The eardrum is vibrating but the mind is attached to the reading. Or some other time you may be listening to some beautiful music. People may be passing by, but you will not notice them.

Pratyāhāra, Withdrawing the Mind from the Senses

Some people sleep with the eyes wide open. Yet they do not see anything. Others are sitting in this lecture, but not one single word will fall into their open ears because their minds are in some other place. They will not remember a single word. Whenever the mind is intensely concentrated on one sense, all the other senses are dead because you cannot connect to their function. This natural ability to withdraw the mind from all the senses and focus them on one area inside is called pratyāhāra in rāja yoga. You do not start directly with the practice of concentration or meditation; you must first learn pratyāhāra. Once you withdraw the mind from the senses, you are not receiving any perception – the senses are not there.

Suppose 10 people walk down a busy urban street. Some people can be seen in shorts, others are wearing hats, and again others are wearing dresses. When these 10 people come back from their outing, you ask them: "What did you see on the main street?" Will they describe the same thing? All had the eyes wide open. One person may say: "I saw the most beautiful hats there." Maybe there is an engineer in the group. He may say "I saw the most beautiful historical building; its architecture is absolutely beautiful." Each one will see only that in which he is interested. The rest was naturally shut off.

This ability is necessary. People need it because day and night innumerable impressions are brought from the senses, from the eyes, the ears, and the nose. This also applies to meditation: without pratyāhāra the mind will remain continuously engaged in countless sensory impressions which will disturb your peace of mind. What we are trying to teach is that you must learn to shut off the mind for a short time every day; for about half-hour to one hour, you should learn to shut off the mind from the senses. This is pratyāhāra.

Amongst the five senses, two senses are very prominent, and they are sight and sound. The remaining senses are not active all the time – they will not bother you too much. Even if the smell of a hot dog comes, you will not be bothered by it. This is not so with sight and sound. We are always alert to those two senses. Among these two major senses, one of them is the core sense, it is more prominent. Which do you prefer, sight or sound? How many people prefer to be blind? How many people would rather be deaf? Generally, there is only a minority of people who want to keep their hearing and would rather lose their eyesight. This also shows in the way people design the method to focus their mind. If you are more sensitive to sight, you will prefer to focus on an object. If you are more sensitive to sound, you would like to focus on a sound. You may focus on sight and concentrate the mind on a candle or the image of Lord Kṛṣṇa, or any other deity, or on the image of a cross. You could also focus on a big hot dog. But will you be able to concentrate? No, it will only take the mind to a lower sensory level. To concentrate the mind, you need a more sublime object than an ordinary hot dog. A person who is playing a game also needs some concentration. Playing the guitar or washing dishes also requires concentration. But this level is not sufficient for the practice of meditation. Therefore, it is better to use a candle flame or an image of Lord Kṛṣṇa. Others will use a sound like *Ram, Shyam, Om Aiṃ Hrīm Klīm, Om Namah Śivaya, Om Namo Nārāyanāya.*

Language and Thought

Now listen to this word: rose flower. Did everybody see a rose flower? If you didn't see a rose flower, it indicates that this word has no meaning for you. Now close your eyes and see a flower, but do not allow the mind to say any name. Is it possible to visualize the flower without its name? This applies also to abstract things, which we cannot see. Now listen: India. What form came? Maybe yogis sitting in meditation. Now listen: Canada. What form came? A maple leaf or some Eskimos? Now listen: Heaven. Nobody has seen heaven, but still, you have some vision of it. Now listen: God. If you are Christian, maybe you think of a man on a throne with a scepter and a crown on his head. Or you see Lord Kṛṣṇa with a flute in his hand. Or you see the dancing Lord Śiva. But for God as Infinity, you cannot think of anything. God as Infinity is formless in nature. The finite mind cannot grasp that infinite God. To reach this infinite state, yogis use the finite mind and concentrate.

The use of Symbols

Let us come back to the example of Canada or simply the city of Vancouver: Nobody has seen every house and every street of the city. To find out what is Canada or Vancouver, you will take a map which will help the mind to have a pinpointed image. You will transfer the infinite Canada into a finite map. The map itself is not Canada, it is only a small piece of paper, but it will guide you to reach there. Without a map you will be lost. In the same way, a name and a form of God like Rāma or Kṛṣṇa or Śiva is like a map which can guide the mind to the infinite. Both name and form should go together. If you start with repeating the name, you will gradually also visualize a form. Or if you focus on a form, then you will repeat the mantra later. Sound and form always go together. Once you can shut off both sight and hearing, then all the senses will come under your control. This is the technique of pratyāhāra in rāja yoga. This needs to be practiced before you can successfully practice concentration and meditation.

THE MONKEY MIND

In India,when people want to catch a monkey, they take a coconut and cut a small hole on the top. Through that hole, some cooked rice is placed inside the coconut. The monkey will put its hand inside and grab the rice by making a fist. The hand could easily move out without making a fist. But the fist is too big to pass through the narrow whole. The monkey will struggle and run with the coconut and try to climb a tree with it. He could easily free itself from the coconut by opening the fist. But once the monkey has caught hold of the food inside the coconut, it will not open the fist.

This illustrates the power of the subconscious mind which does not allow us to let go of our habits. We will not become independent and free, unless we ask the questions: who am I, where do I come from, what is my purpose here?

Just for two minutes, draw all the senses inwards. Bring the mind to the center, the Self. Shut off all the senses. Breathe very gently in and out and repeat the cosmic sound OM. Your mind will settle down. Then peace and strength will come to you automatically. All the strength is within you. You lost your peace and strength because you followed the instinctive mind, the subconscious mind. Meditate now and reach your real freedom. That freedom is within you.

MIND OVER MEDICINE – EMERGENCY MEDICINE IN HIMALAYAN SECLUSION

In early 1950 I lived for some time in a remote part of the Himalayas known as Uttar Kashi, practicing yoga and meditation. I obtained permission from my beloved spiritual Master H. H. Sri Swami Sivanandaji Maharaj and left the Sivananda Ashram in Rishikesh, at the foot of the Himalayas, to go into the interior and higher altitudes of the Himalayas. The high altitude and the majestic snow-clad Himalayan peaks brought me the natural elevating atmosphere for my Yogic practices.

At that time, I never thought I would come face to face with the problems of another human being. I was just 20 and in the best of health. Moreover, it was my training period, and I used to spend many hours in prāṇāyāma, relaxation, dhyāna (meditation), and in doing all of the 84 difficult yogic āsanas as well as hundreds of variations, and all the kriyās or yogic cleansing exercises. My mind was peaceful. During prāṇāyāma, mysterious movements of prāṇa would energize my body to a point where I felt sometimes, I could lift the whole world. At that time, I forgot all about disease and pain.

During this training period, an old man from a remote mountain village trekked miles to my cottage for medical help. He had a fever and a very painful headache. There was no one within miles of his village who could medically assist to relieve his suffering; this is very common in remote areas of India. Naturally, a holy man, a swami, was the next best thing to be found. But when I went to meditate in solitude, I never thought I would be thrown into a situation where an utterly helpless human being would come for medical aid from a young and inexperienced man like me. I had a good knowledge of physiology and anatomy and had taken some first aid courses, but how was I to remove the headache, fever and pain from a helpless man who put all his trust in a swami?

I did not have any first aid kit or any aspirin because I had thought it would not be necessary for me. I was as helpless as he was. So, I invented a miracle medicine, which I thought would work. The old man was illiterate, but he had faith in swamis like me and holy men, though I never thought or intended to be one. I thought that medicine could be created from his mere faith in my spiritual powers.

I went into my cottage leaving the old man outside, assuring him that I would be back soon with some miraculous medicine, the way he expected from a holy swami.

I had no choice now except to create the illusory medicine. I went to my meditation room, took a glass of water, added two teaspoons of milk from my meagre ration for that day, to change the color of the water, and added a teaspoon of sugar and a few drops of lemon juice to create a taste for the medicine. Now my concoction or medicine compound had a distinctive grey color with a sugar and lemon taste which I thought was sure to convince the old man about the miraculous medicine. In a ceremonial way I stirred the mixture with a shining silver-like spoon in front of the old man. After OM chanting and a prayer to Lord Śiva, I gave the instant medicine to the old man with the assurance that he would be alright within half an hour, the time necessary for the medicine to penetrate his blood stream and relieve the pain.

The old man drank the water, and I made him rest under the shade of a tree, covered by his tattered blanket. Believe it or not, within a half hour his headache had gone. I put my hand on his forehead to check his feverish condition, and my hand thermometer assured me that the temperature had come down. Faith, the miraculous wonder drug, man's oldest medicine, had worked again. The old man was extremely happy over my spiritual power as well as the knowledge of modern medicine I possessed, as he knew I was educated in a western way. But I was disappointed about my spiritual powers and my western education because I knew that this cure had taken place only through faith. If I had an aspirin, I would have given it to that old man instead of my sugar lemon water. But I doubt that aspirin would have worked at all if he had thought it a worthless medicine.

My story of emergency medicine in the Himalayas seems to be something of a fairytale. Maybe, but it worked. Is it not so that all medicines, whether it is aspirin or cold pills, work like a fairytale? Is something missing in our theory or perception about man, mind, and medicine? When the old man walked away from my Himalayan cottage, I understood that all medicine and cures are in the mind of the individual only. The external medicine, whether it is an aspirin, or holy water from my puja room are only a crutch for the mind so that it can draw its own unlimited power from within.

For the past 20 years I have been living in America, amongst the wealthiest and most educated people on earth, the opposite of the type of illiterate people I used to live with in the remote mountains. But I see the same ignorance in the so-called educated people of America. Just as the villager had absolute faith in a holy man like me, so also the average educated American man has faith in his doctor, psychiatrist, and Madison Avenue advertisers who tell him what product he should eat, what brand of cigarettes he should smoke, which tranquilizer is best, which sleeping pill will give him or her the best sleep. On the sole assurance that it has been advertised as "enriched bread" in national magazines, people will buy a brand of white bread – stripped of all its vitamin contents – as being suitable for their children's youth and strength.

Mind is the greatest force on this earth. He who has controlled his mind, is full of power. The first sign of the real intellect is noted with the dawn of self-consciousness, or self-awareness. With this self-consciousness, man begins to rely more upon his mind rather than blindly accepting that which comes from others. It is through the unfoldment of the intellect that man receives more and more light from the next higher phase of the mind, the higher mind. Even these little rays of the higher mind can help us to awaken into our spiritual consciousness, though it may be several lives before we attain full spiritual consciousness or universal consciousness.

BONDAGE AND FREEDOM

In yoga there is a saying:
mana eva manuṣyāṇāṁ kāraṇaṁ bandhamokṣayoḥ

"Mind alone is the cause of bondage and freedom for human beings." (Amritabindu Upanishad, verse 2)

This can be compared to a ladder. It takes you up to a height. But if you are careless, you fall and break your head. The same ladder can take you up or bring injury or even death. Through the practice of yoga, you can train the mind so that it will take you up. Ordinary people don't train the mind. They are being controlled by their emotions. There are seven basic emotions: lust, anger, greed, hatred, jealousy, envy, and fear. Fear is the most damaging emotion. It contracts all our existence, our life. When there is fear, you will not be able to climb up the ladder properly.

Imaginary Fears

There are real fears and imaginary fears. Imaginary fears are called anxiety. Here are some examples of anxiety or imaginary fear:

- I am sitting here, but now and then I am looking up. Why? There is only a very remote chance that the ceiling will fall. But nevertheless, I am afraid that the ceiling will fall on my head. This is an imaginary fear.
- While using an elevator, I am afraid that I will get stuck.
- If you are a mother or a father and your son or daughter went out to a dance party, and it is ten o'clock or ten thirty and your child is not back home. You think that he or she is supposed to be here at ten thirty, maybe there was an accident.

Then there are imaginary fears which are necessary for our health and happiness:

- When the father or the mother gently throws the baby up into the air and then brings it down in a playful mood, the baby is not afraid. But if a stranger like me tries to do that, it will be different. The baby's imaginary instinct says there is a danger because I don't know this man. I cannot trust him. Though the baby cannot even talk, the instinct is working.
- Or let us put a plank at a height of two feet from here to the end of the hall. You all will be easily able to walk over the plank from here to there. But if the same plank is positioned at a height of eight feet, then it is different. For the muscles it is the same work. But a height of eight feet is dangerous unless you are a circus person.

These are examples of imaginary positive fear. All types of fear stop our progress. Fear is a specific wave of the mind. Patanjali explains this in the yoga Sutras: "yoga is stopping all types of waves of the mind."

Moods and Emotions

When emotional waves are very high, this will not only destroy your peace of mind but will also bring about physiological conditions. Emotions have two degrees or intensities, higher and lower. In the lower intensity they are called moods. For example, there is an angry mood and then there is actual anger.

The wife is supposed to make supper for her husband at seven o'clock. The husband is waiting. It is seven o'clock and she has not come. He will turn the television on, waiting for her to come for supper. Half an hour. Seven thirty. She is not back. Eight o'clock, eight thirty, nine o'clock!! Now when she comes home, the whole ceiling may fall. First it was just a small wave: ok, maybe she will come in twenty minutes. It is just an angry mood. But once it is actual anger it can become so extreme that you will shoot or stab a person. Your reason stops functioning. That is called temporary madness. It can happen to any of us.

Another example: the wife has been vacuuming and cleaning the whole house. Then the husband comes home, lights a cigarette, and drops ash on the floor. She is already tired and exhausted and here comes that ash on the carpet. Now there will be flying saucers in the house. That's when an angry mood becomes actual anger.

Or the wife returns home from shopping, and she has made a dent on the new car. The husband also just returns from the office. He is in a splendid mood because his salary was just increased. The wife says "Honey, I made a dent in the car." As he is in a happy mood, he replies: "Don't worry about it, we will take care of it."

We always look at the other person's mood. A child wants something from the parents, for example a bicycle and says, "mommy, mommy, tell daddy I want a bicycle." Mommy looks at her husband's face and replies to the child: "Not now. He's not in a good mood." In the same way, the husband wants to ask something from his wife, but he waits for her to be in a good mood. Whether we call someone a friend or an enemy, your perception will depend on how you think, on how your mood is. You may get angry at a friend if you are in a bad mood. We all have moods. These moods will affect our nervous system and our endocrine system. They can even affect the physical body in the form of faulty postural alignment. If you are constantly worrying about something, you will be automatically contracting many muscles in the shoulder and neck area. After some time, you will feel pain radiating to your hands. This is one of the reasons why āsanas or postures are practiced: they release this tension. We should learn how to counteract these moods.

When I came here tonight, I did not directly start talking to you. Imagine for a moment that you are all business people and I want to speak to you about business. Then I would put my hands in my pockets, stand in front of you and speak with this attitude. But here, we create a spiritual mood. We sat in silence, we repeated OM, and suddenly the atmosphere is charged with a positive energy, a positive mood. I can tune to you very easily now and you can tune to me. Again, suppose I would stand with my hands in my pocket and talk to you, that would not be the right mood. You would not like to hear my talk if I would be in that state of mind.

Stress and the Fight or Flight Mechanism

Whether we know it or not, the circumstances of daily live constantly affect our mood. This reaction is called the fight or flight mechanism. We have inherited it from our ancestors in the forest. They had to face real dangers like a tiger coming or some other animal attacking them. If you would be in the forest and heard a tiger nearby, what would you do? You might run away from there, that is called flight. Or if there is no time to run, then you would have to fight to survive. In the nervous system, this is called the fight or flight mechanism. It is necessary for our survival. At that time even a lame man will have the strength to run faster because his life is in danger. The same mechanism operates whether we are living in the forest or in a city apartment. It affects the autonomous nervous system, which means it is an involuntary, automatic reaction.

You are cooking dinner in the kitchen and the phone rings in the living room. You cannot leave the kitchen, otherwise the food will burn. The moment the phone rings your muscles become tight. You think, maybe my daughter will answer the phone. You wait. But the phone keeps ringing, and nobody is answering the call. The tension increases. Finally, the phone stops ringing. But is the crisis over now? The fight or flight mechanism was activated automatically without your knowledge. Therefore, the muscle tension will continue until you do some walking or running or some other exercise. Often things happen simultaneously. The phone crisis may be over but now you touch the hot stove. You try to find a band-aid and continue cooking at the same time. At that moment the phone starts ringing again and simultaneously your child starts crying in the next room. Where do you go? Do you attend the dinner, the finger, the phone, or the crying child? Now the fight or flight mechanism has reached an intense stage.

These things happen every day, is it not? What do ordinary people do to release these tensions? Finally, supper is over, and you are watching the television. There you see terrorists blowing up an embassy and people are dying. This further activates the fight or flight mechanism. You switch the channel and watch a football game. Your favorite team is playing, and you are anxious that your team should win the game. Tension builds up further. It is now 11pm. Throughout the day your body has accumulated tensions and is waiting for a release. But you opened the television and became further agitated. To cope, you pour a drink and smoke some cigarettes while watching the television. Then you lie down in your soft bed. The muscles are contracted but you are not aware of it while you sleep for eight hours. Then you get up, but the muscles are still in a contracted and painful state.

Again, you light a cigarette and drink coffee. You heart starts pumping faster. Then you comb your hair and put on a shirt, tie, pants, and a coat. You drive your car through rush hour traffic. Have you seen anyone rushing during rush hour time? Nobody is rushing. You just sit in the standing car, looking at other cars on all four sides. You smoke another cigarette, while you are also inhaling the pollution of the traffic jam. You reach the office late and your boss is angry. Then after a whole day of work you return home, and your wife is telling you that she made a dent in the car. Do you understand the condition of our life? Whether we are ordinary people or the president of a country, we are all in the same state. We don't know what to do.

Now you understand the importance of yoga. Yogis know this tension. When they get up in the morning, they try to create a positive mood. They repeat OM, then meditate on inner peace and then chant some mantras. This silences the mind.

MEDITATION

PLEASURE, PAIN, AND BLISS

We constantly experience pain and pleasure, but not bliss. We will try to find out what bliss is and how to find it. First let us analyze two experiences in which we find ourselves continuously. These are the experiences of pain and pleasure. What is pleasure for one person is pain for another person. If pleasure is an objective reality, then we must get the experience of the pleasure equally, without any difference. If the pleasure coming from the senses is real, then we all must get the same experience, from the senses, is it not? But this is not the case. We do not have a common sense experience.

Sensory Experience Happens in the Brain

Let's say I put my right hand into extremely cold water and the left hand into quite hot water. After a few minutes I put both hands it into 20°C water. The left hand is coming from the experience of ice-cold water. What will it say? Oh, this 20°C water is very warm. And the right hand, which is coming from hot water, will say, oh this is cold. I am having these two experiences simultaneously. Which experience is right? Which experience are you going to accept?

Scientists say that it is possible that experiences of

pleasure and pain can be created simply by stimulating certain brain centers. You put a hot dog into your mouth where it creates a beautiful and pleasant sensation. What is the process? The hot dog creates a taste by stimulating the taste buds. From the taste buds, tiny nerves carry these impulses to the brain center, and it is there that the effect of pleasure is created. Scientists can stimulate brain centers directly with small electrodes and suddenly you get the most pleasant experience of tasting a beautiful dinner or of hearing beautiful music. You can even change emotions and habits through electrical stimulation of the brain. An experiment was conducted where an electrode was implanted into the brain of a bull. The bull was about to attack the scientists. But when the scientists turned on the small electrode, an electronic gadget just like you would use to turn on your television, the bull became gentle like a pussy cat. In this way, mental moods can be changed. Maybe sometime in the future, a government may put electrodes into everyone's brains. Then the masses can be controlled by turning one switch, and everybody will behave like a pussy cat.

The sensation of pleasure is only nerve impulse. It can be compared to scratching. When there is an itch and you start scratching, how does it feel? First it feels so good, but if you keep on scratching, it burns. Now the experience turns from pleasure into pain. In the same way, all pleasure is just an illusion created by your mind, it is not reality. It can be produced through your senses, through hypnotism, through control of your mind, or through electronic impulses sent to different areas of the brain. Pleasure is only in your mind. It is not a permanent reality.

Beyond Pleasure and Pain

And not only is it not a permanent reality, but pleasure also always ends in pain. That is a law. The first scratching feels good, but continue and it becomes painful. A king-size cigarette will bring king size cancer. Drinking big bottles of champagne will affect the liver, it will look horrible like a hamburger. That is the reaction, nobody can escape that law.

Moreover, your senses cannot support the experience of pleasure for long. When the pleasant experience continues for a long time, it will become irritating or boring. It can be compared to moving a muscle. For the first few minutes you can exercise, but as you continue to move the same muscles, they get tired. So also, your senses get tired of any experience. Can you take even the most amazing sensory experience for 24 hours? Even if the experience involves no pain at all, can you bear it for 24 hours? It is the same with emotional experiences, can you take it for 24 hours? Can you love your husband or wife passionately for 24 hours? No matter how much you love him or her, after some time you just want to be alone in peace and silence.

"Please leave me alone" – who is here who has not said these words? But who understood the meaning of this sentence? It shows that something is there in that lonely state which is blissful. There is nothing which is going to disturb me. The experience of having objects or money, sensual experiences, emotional experiences, none of these experiences can substitute the experience of being alone.

Continue to indulge in sense pleasure and there are always consequences. Nobody can escape that law.

Pain and pleasure are both subjective, depending upon your state of mind. Pleasure becomes pain and pain become pleasure. Due to this kind of adverse reaction, pleasure and pain are called pairs of opposites. But bliss is different from both pain and pleasure. It is the state of bliss alone, which is not related to anything except the all-pervading Self, the "I am".

Leaving the Waking State

Can I remain in the experience "I am Swami Vishnu-devananda, a yoga teacher, sitting on a pillow before all of you" all the time? Can I think of the Yoga Camp and other ashrams and centers all the time? Can I talk about yoga and be a yoga teacher all the time? Sometimes I want to forget all of this.

Does this also occur to you? Would you like to stay all the time in the experience of husband or wife, father or mother, son or daughter, or of prime minister or president of the United States, or judge or professor, or male or female? Would you be able to remain in the waking state experience for 24 hours? It doesn't matter how pleasant it is, you cannot carry on with it after some time. You want to forget the experience of this waking reality. We can see that there is not only a natural limit to the experience of pleasure and pain, but also to the entire waking state. The waking state is living one type of cosmic illusion. There is a need in everyone to regularly leave this waking reality behind.

The Dream State

Then comes the second state, the dream state. In dream there are also experiences of pleasure and pain but no experience of bliss. The dream experience is as true as the waking state and as false as the waking state. Suppose someone gave you a golden bed. When you try to sleep in this golden bed, you are only thinking about the golden bed instead of falling asleep. Finally, you give the golden bed away and find a sleeping bag and sleep in a tent. The purpose of a bed is to forget the bed itself. You want to forget the waking reality. The mind feels punished in the waking reality because it is under many constraints. I must act in a certain way. I must act like a swami, you must act like a husband, or a wife and follow many rigid rules which were created by the society. You must use the phone in certain way, you must us the fork in a certain way.

When the mind enters the dream, it acts just like a child let loose after school. The mind now does not want to follow any rigid rules. It can create its own rules and regulations. Now the mind can eat the food it likes, according to its own fantasies. But nobody can live in this fantasy all the time either. The dream fantasies of pleasure and pain also create stress and strain.

Deep Sleep

Now you want to enter the third state, the deep sleep state. All we remember from deep sleep is that it was a good sleep. But there is a difference between the unconscious state and deep sleep. In the unconscious state the mind is paralyzed. But in deep sleep there is awareness of something.

Something is common in the waking state and the dream state. In both states, there are objects which you experience. There can be a pizza in the waking state and there can be a pizza in the dream state. Both are experienced with the senses. There is sense experience also in the dream state: you can see, hear, taste, smell, and touch in your dream. The physical senses are not active, yet there is sense experience. Also, both in the waking and the dream state, the mind must be present and connected with the senses. Sensual experience is possible only when the mind is in contact with the senses. When the mind is not connected to the senses, then there is no sensual experience.

A scientist is working on a laboratory experiment. Due to his concentration, he is not aware of his surroundings. Maybe next door there is a fire alarm and fire fighters are entering the building, but he will be in the laboratory just concentrating on his experiment without being aware of the situation next door. The mind must be connected to the five senses. Only then experience is possible.

Object, Senses, Mind and "I am"

Three things are necessary for the experience of pleasure or pain: object, senses and mind. Experience depends on the mental state whether these experiences are going to be pleasant or unpleasant. It does not depend on the object. If the experience would be in the object, then you would always have the same experience. But this is not the case. You are enjoying a nice dinner with family and friends. Everyone is enjoying the delicious dishes. At that moment you receive a phone call, informing you that a close friend had an accident and is admitted to the hospital, seriously injured. Will the food still be tasty? All interest for dinner stopped, because the mind is no longer interested in the sensual experience.

There is an object, there are senses, there is the mind and then there is a fourth element: that is the experiencer, which we call "I am". Both in the waking and the dream state, these four things are present. In the deep sleep state, something is missing: there is no object to experience, there are no senses to perceive anything and there is no mind. These three things are absent. What is left is the "I am". This is what we refer to when we say: "Leave me alone".

Is there any difference between my deep sleep experience and your deep sleep experience? I am a swami from India and practice meditation yoga since age 17. Should my deep sleep experience therefore be different from your deep sleep experience? No, everyone has the same deep sleep experience. One woman is talking the whole day about women's' liberation and there is a man who is talking about men's liberation. Both go into deep sleep. In that state, do they know whether they are a woman or a man? Their experience is the same. They lost their gender identity. A man with terminal cancer and terrible pain, a woman with serious heart problems, a man who just made a profit of ten thousand dollars in the stock market, and a woman who just got married: they all enter the deep sleep state. Whose deep sleep is superior? Both pleasure and pain disappear in the deep sleep state.

In the deep sleep, there is only peace and bliss, there is only the experience of "I am". There is no mind to experience any objects, there are no senses functioning. There is only the experience of being alone. Deep sleep is exactly opposite to both the waking and the dream state. In both the waking and the dream state, there is duality. In deep sleep there is no duality, only the experience of I am. The bliss of the deep sleep state is due to the experience of "I am".

The problem is that when I come out of deep sleep into the waking state, I am the same old fool: Again, I think that I am Swami Vishnudevananda, the yoga teacher. I think that I own this house and that I have so many students. I am so proud. I am a great man. Another person will say: I am the president, I am a businessman, I am a professor, I am a housewife, I am a husband, I am a saint, I am a sinner.

What is common in all these statements? It is the words "I am". And this common part cannot be changed. I am, period. The problem is that we forget this "I am". We identify with the qualities: yoga teacher, husband, wife, yogi, saint, sinner, king, president. When we identify with these qualities instead of the "I am", only then there comes pleasure and pain. When there is pleasure and pain you are still experiencing the "I am", but you are not identifying with it. Instead, you are identifying with the objective qualities. That is why pain and pleasure exist. That is why there is dissatisfaction amongst all of us.

Instead of sitting here on the hard floor, you could have gone to some other place for a more pleasing sensual experience. Instead, you choose to come here, because you want to hear about peace which is different than pleasure and pain. This peace is also called the fourth state, beyond the three states of waking, dreaming and deep sleep. This ultimate bliss experience is called samādhi, superconscious or transcendental state.

The Transcendental Experience

Deep sleep and this transcendental experience have something in common, just like the waking and the dream state have something in common. The duality of subject and the object is common for both the waking and dream state. And what is common for both the deep sleep and the transcendental state is the experience of non-duality or "I am". Yet in deep sleep this experience of "I am" is covered by the veil of ignorance. A red veil in front of a light bulb makes the true white light appear as red. If the veil is black, no light comes through at all. In deep sleep you come close to the "I am".

You are that "I"; there is no object. But it is covered by a veil which is like black paper. The veil prevents us from obtaining the full impression of the "I".

The transcendental experience is just like deep sleep, only the veil is removed, so the "I am" can be experienced. Moses heard a voice in the burning bush. The voice said, "I am that I am". The voice did not say "I am God, I am the Supreme Being". It only said, "I am that I am". Jesus proclaimed the same when he said: "I am He". Neither Moses nor Jesus said "I am this body, this mind or this object". They only said "I am". I am existence. I am knowledge. I am bliss. That transcendental experience is like deep sleep, a non-dual experience where there is no pain at all. It is all bliss.

Not only is there no pain, but the bliss is also infinite, it is ultimate bliss. It is compared to fire and heat. Suppose you take the heat out of the fire, then there is no more fire. The heat is the inherent quality of fire. Heat and fire are one and the same. Just like fire is not experiencing heat, but it is heat itself, similarly I am not experiencing bliss, but I am bliss. That is why there are no words to speak about it to anybody.

If a person in deep sleep is asked "hey, are you sleeping?" Then the person replies "Yes, I am sleeping", it proves that the person is not sleeping. So also, a person in bliss cannot say to anybody I am experiencing bliss. But when he or she comes out of that state, there is a new understanding. It is like being awake for the first time, seeing the world became an illusion. I thought there was pleasure and happiness in this world, but it is just an illusion, and that illusion is now gone. The remembrance of that bliss is so powerful that there cannot be any more worry about pain or pleasure. Once a person comes from the transcendental experience, he or she is always happy. Still the person must work through karma; there are karmic debts. But these karmic debts are experienced like a Hitchcock movie.

Identification with Illusion

Two people watch a Hitchcock movie, one cries, and the other person is watching it just like an illusion. Many people got very scared when they watch the movie *The Exorcist*. My uncle was a great mantra vadi, he would perform exorcism with certain mantras. I have seen myself the presence of actual spirits and how he would pray and make them leave the person. However, when the movie *The Exorcist*. was produced, there was no actual spirit. I was interested in seeing how the movie would create the illusion of exorcism, which made people scream. So I went to see it. It is a double illusion: **1)** the movie was shot in a studio with actors, there was no spirit. **2)** when it is projected on the silver screen of the movie theatre, there is just a play of light and shadows.

Our experiences are no different from a movie. We go to the movie for entertainment in the form of a painful or a pleasant experience. The painful experience of a Hitchcock movie is also entertainment. You see now how the mind wants both pleasant as well as unpleasant experiences. You want these experiences even if you know that they are an illusion. In the same way, māyā creates the illusion of this world which is continuously changing. The mind experiences the changing world as individual frames. You are seeing only individual frames of this world and then your mind puts it together as if it was a movie. You saw the most beautiful wedding, a very pleasant experience. Then you hear that the couple got divorced. The wife gave everything to him, but he ran away from her and got married to someone else. Now you are projecting a different feeling through your mind.

The painful illusion of the movie *The Exorcist* is caused by what? It is not caused by reality. It is caused by your mind. Your mind wants to experience horror. When I saw the movie, I did not have any emotion; I was only thinking how they created the film. I was not screaming. I did not lose my identity. I knew that I am Swami Vishnudevananda. I knew that there was only a white screen. I did not merge with that movie object and experience it. I was watching and witnessing the whole presentation, knowing all the time who I am. But other people were affected because they lost their identity and started identifying with the false image, the illusion.

Bliss can be experienced by identifying with the "I am", while watching this world moving on. In fact, there is no husband, wife, children and so forth. These exist only in your mind. You are walking on the street; suddenly you see a girl and you fall in love. Honey, I love you. She says: oh, honey I love you too. You get married. Now when you laugh, she also laughs and when she cries, you also cry. Oh honey, I will sacrifice everything for you. And the next day you want to sacrifice her. The person is the same but your mind changes. Suppose she decides to live with another man, what do you want to do now? You want to kill her. It shows that you did not love her for her sake. Your experience was that she is my girl, my wife. This is an illusion. She is still an individual person. Even after marrying her, she still must eat, she must sleep, she must find her own happiness. What makes the difference when you say that you are married to her, is that you said she is mine. That is your illusion, not her illusion. If she says that he is my husband, then she is also in her own illusion. This my-ness creates the problem of pain and pleasure. The idea "she is my wife, and he is my husband" exists only in your mind. This house is my yoga centre because I signed a paper. But literally it belongs to the mortgage company. It is the idea of my-ness which creates pain and pleasure. We need to get out of these objects and the my-ness. Only then we see the "I am" in the transcendental state, which is all bliss.

This big Hitchcock movie which is this world is called "māyā" in Sanskrit. Māyā creates this huge movie for us and projects it through the individual mind. The individual mind is the screen, each of us carries his or her individual television program in the head. Māyā is the cosmic transmitter. She transmits a play and according to your channel, your illusion is created. Each one of us is watching a different channel. One channel is a Hitchcock movie, and we cry, next door another person is laughing because he or she is on another channel. In the movie of māyā, the actor is the mind. The mind can project its own play and at the same time visualize the play. The mind has an infinite number of channels. Each channel can make us forgot our true identity. Yogis come and say this is the plight of the māyā. If you want to be happy, look only in one place, in the "I am". The Kingdom of heaven is within in the "I am". The "I am" is the only real substance. Everything else is false.

In conclusion: You have three experiences – waking, dreaming and deep sleep. Both in the waking and the dream state there is pain and pleasure, because there are objects, senses, mind and the experiencer, or the "I am". In deep sleep the objects do not exist. If pain and pleasure would be real, then we must have pain all the time or pleasure all the time. But sometimes pain becomes pleasure, and pleasure becomes pain. The pain and pleasure of the waking or the dream state both disappear in the deep sleep state. There is no pain nor pleasure, there is only an awareness of peace and bliss. But still there is ignorance.

Peace – the Missing Experience

If you are satisfied with your life, then you don't have to search any further. Then you would not have come here. Something is missing in your life, it doesn't matter how much money you have, what kind of home you have. In all of us there is a vacuum, and when the vacuum is intense, you start seeking. Though there is a vacuum in everybody's heart, only a few people can realize this vacuum as painful, as an experience like hunger. It is hunger for an experience of silence, of peace without any external world. You want to be alone. That experience of being alone is possible only in a transcendental experience when you can stop the play of the mind. The play of the mind feeds the illusion, this cosmic māyā, and projects this illusion as a reality. When we identify with this illusion, we forget our real nature and are suffering.

Ten friends went on a pilgrimage and had to cross a river. There was no boat, so they decided to swim across. On the other side they wanted to make sure that all arrived safely. The leader starts counting, but one is missing. The second leader counted. Again, one is missing. Everyone started counting and each one found only nine. The tenth person was missing, and they did not know who this tenth person was. They were crying. Now a stranger came by and said: let me count. He counted ten people. Who was the missing person? The person who was counting didn't count himself. So, for whom they were crying? For him or herself.

Materially speaking, America is the heaven on this earth. All material things are there. Top intellects, technology, science. America sent a man to the moon and at the same time carpet bombed Cambodia. But what happened to peace? You cannot find it externally, and you also cannot find it at home, so you came here searching. The pain of the missing peace has brought you here. And that is why yoga is popular. But there is also a danger here because this vacuum and your search attracts lots of peddlers. They know that there is some weakness because you are searching. They can easily sell things which are not real.

The Way to Peace

Yoga is not something new. It cannot be concocted, nor is it me who brought yoga. It is a subject known from time immemorial. No-one has changed the technique of meditation, of finding inner peace or silence. It is all given already. The masters only pass it on from teacher to disciples. For thousands of years this subject and its techniques did not change. I am not telling anything new to you. This subject is not mine. It is an experience of thousands of people before. An experience I also had and which I am sharing with you. If you want this experience, you will have to practice. I cannot give the experience to you.

Nobody can taste honey for you. If you want to know the taste of honey, you will have to taste it on your own. If you never tasted honey or any other sweet taste, and I am telling you about honey, will it give you the actual taste? Honey is a carbohydrate sweet. It tastes like sugar. It is very sweet and pleasant. Would these two intellectual theories or any other scientific aspects of honey convey the taste to you? There are no words to convey the taste because it is an experience. In the same way this inner experience of "I am" is only possible when there is a vacuum. Then you must search in the right place within you, in that "I", in that missing person which you are yourself. What is missing, is the "I am".

THE EXPERIENCE OF INNER SILENCE

The experience when you still the mind, cannot be explained. Yogis explain it only through negation. Not this, not that. In Sanskrit, it is explained like this:

na antaḥ prajña,
na bahiṣ prajña
na ubhayatas prajña
na prajnāna ghanaṃ
na prajnaṃ nāprajña
adṛṣṭam, avyavahārvam, agrāhya
alakṣaṇam, acintyam

(Mandukya Upanishad, verse 7)

na antahprajña: It is not an experience which you get inside when you close your eyes or when you think of your wife or children.
na bahiṣ prajña: Nor the experience when you watch a beautiful sunset or a beautiful scene or a beautiful body, etc., that is not the experience.
na ubhayatas prajña: Not any in-between experience also.
adṛṣṭam: Whatever is seen is not that experience.
avyavahārvam: You cannot imagine that experience.
agrāhya: You cannot grasp that experience. You cannot grasp it and put it on a paper or it into a computer.
alakṣaṇam: There is no comparison to that experience. "Oh yes, that experience is like this experience" – no, you cannot compare it, there is no comparison.
acintyam: You cannot even think about it. Even the greatest novelist or fiction writer cannot even imagine what those experiences are.

We are incapable of expressing that peace or silence or bliss or happiness. That is the experience when you still the mind. Yoga is trying to stop the thought waves which disturb your mental peace or happiness. Happiness is not outside, it is not inside either, but where is it then? You are that happiness, we call it ānanda. Just like a candle, if I touch it, it will burn my hand. Heat and fire are one and the same. You take the heat out of fire, then it is not fire. The inherent nature of fire is heat. Heat and fire are one and the same. In the same way, your Self and bliss, ānanda are one and the same. They are not separate things.

Why can you not find that happiness? Because there are disturbances in the mind, waves, thought waves. Once you stop these thought waves, you find who you are. Then you understand that peace. "I understand that peace now" – you cannot say that because in that inner peace, there is no duality. You become subject and object. There is no difference between knower, knowledge and the known. There is no difference between experiencer, experienced and the experience. That's why the Bible speaks about "the peace that passes all understanding". Because in that peaceful state of the mind, you merge into the eternal silence. That's called immortality. That's called superconscious state. That's called God realization or Self-realization. You are aware of the Self, you realize I am the Self. Self-realization is the goal and that is possible only when you silence the thoughts.

QUESTIONS AND ANSWERS

THE MANY ASPECTS OF YOGA

This interview was conducted at the occasion of the presentation of the *New Book of Yoga* published by the Sivananda Yoga Vedanta Centre London in the spring of 1983.

For several decades the book was published as:

The Book of Yoga – Step by Step Guide
The New Book of Yoga
The Sivananda Companion to Yoga

Question: Swamiji, could you tell us what prompted you to bring yoga to the West originally?

Answer: My master said "people are waiting". This is true because many Eastern souls are reincarnating now in the West, in Europe and in America. Yoga is not new to them. They already know this subject from a past life. I came to reawaken their past memory and bring them back to their spiritual life so they can proceed further on the spiritual path.

When I came to America in 1957, yoga was practically unknown. I travelled and gave television and radio programs, public demonstrations and lectures in universities and colleges. The *Complete Illustrated Book of Yoga* was published. It explains things in a more modern scientific way and helped the West to understand what true yoga means. Yoga has become very popular. Many universities and other places are conducting yoga classes.

The present tension of life in the West is far beyond the ordinary human being's control. Thousands and thousands of people are living with tranquilizers, sleeping pills, amphetamines to wake up and alcohol because they are unable to cope with the stress. Yoga helps to bring stress under control, not only on the physical level, but also on the mental and spiritual levels. Yoga helps a person to lead a healthy life free of many problems which ordinary people face.

But even then, there is a vacuum inside. This vacuum is caused by a lack of inner peace, an inability to find "the peace that passes all understanding", as the Bible describes it. That's what meditation does. In meditation there are different aspects, different stages for different types of people.

The main cause for the level of stress which the West is facing is the lack of discipline, due to too much excitement. Bars and television, etc, everything excites. There are very few films which bring peace and calm to the mind. Yesterday I saw the movie "Gandhi". It's a beautiful example. Entertainment should calm the emotions and bring our mind under control. That was the teaching of Gandhi. That's the teaching of yoga. In fact, Gandhi was a true Yogi.

Question: What is the importance of haṭha yoga, of doing āsanas?

Answer: Many people think that haṭha yoga consists merely of practicing āsanas. That is a big mistake. Haṭha yoga is the practical aspect of rāja yoga. Both rāja yoga and haṭha yoga consist of the same eight steps: yama, niyama, āsana, prāṇāyāma, pratyāhāra, dhāraṇa, dhyāna, and samādhi. Āsanas come as the third step. It is only a kindergarten lesson.

Next is prāṇāyāma, not only physical breathing but also psychic breathing. It consists of controlling the psychic nerves. After that comes the actual meditation technique. Haṭha yoga is the practical aspect of rāja yoga. Rāja yoga itself does not teach these practical steps; it is haṭha yoga which gives the techniques.

Haṭha yoga means "Ha" and "Ṭha". "Ha" means sun, "Ṭha" means moon, or positive and negative energy. In Chinese this Ha and Ṭha is called Ying and Yang. When these two energies are brought together there is an awakening of energy and consciousness. Normally a person's energy and consciousness move towards a sensual and sexual level. But once the Ha and Ṭha, these two energies are brought together, the energy moves up. Higher centers will open and when the energy reaches the highest center called sahasrāra cakra, then there will be union, which is the aim of yoga. Haṭha yoga is not just some exercise, it is union of Ha and Ṭha. Exercise is just one part and is practiced to obtain control over the physical system.

Question: Can you explain the meaning of prāṇa?

Answer: Yes, it's a word which does not exist in Western terminology. Before Newton, there was no belief in gravity. But gravity was not invented by Newton. He discovered its existence and shared this discovery along with the word gravity. In a similar way, prāṇa is a word for universal energy which manifests in all animate and inanimate beings from the lowest to the highest.

Just look at this beautiful flower. Its beauty consists of the life force which it emanates. It is possible to take a kirlian photograph of a flower which shows the life force emanating from the flower as well as from the leaves. If we take this leaf and take a kirlian photograph of it, we can see that it is not dead. Life is still there in the form of an energy pattern. If the leaf is now divided into halves, and only one half is put on the kirlian photographic plate, the full leaf will still be seen as an energy pattern. Kirlian photography can show the energy pattern or prāṇa even without the presence of the physical leaf.

When you look at a dead body, you do not feel like touching it, even though it may have just stopped breathing. Because there is something missing, and that is the prāṇa. Prāṇa is not the soul. It is an energy just like electricity or the gravitational force. It manifests through this body which is made up of ice cream, pizza, and bananas. When the prāṇa is present, you can see how the body shines. Just like a bulb itself cannot shine without electrical current behind it, in the same way, behind this body, which is made up of food, there is the prāṇa energy.

It is that prāṇa which makes my hand move, my eyes sparkle, and my thoughts to connect to another person's mind. This is all prāṇa. Prāṇa is life giving energy. Some people have a tremendous amount of prāṇa. It is stored in the solar plexus. When this battery is discharged, then there is little prāṇa, the eyes are dim, the verbal expressions are not clear, even though the person may speak in a beautiful language. Yet the words will not cause much impression in others.

This is very different in a person whose thoughts and words are charged with pranic energy. The life work and the personality of a person depend on how much prāṇa he or she has. A tremendous personality can move the world. The achievements of Mahatma Gandhi and many other people are all due to their tremendous prāṇa.

Many people have a good amount of prāṇa, but they may misuse it for sexual pleasures. This dissipates the energy and there is nothing left for them. Prāṇa is the energy which we try to control through the practice of haṭha yoga.

Question: How can you increase or free the flow of prāṇa by the practice of yoga?

Answer: You can easily feel this because there is a reaction in the nervous system, in your spinal cord. During specific breathing exercises the prāṇa will flow upward. Sometimes it creeps like an ant, sometimes it is just like the tingling sensation of an electrical current passing through the cellular system. It magnetizes and energizes your whole body. You feel very peaceful, and meditation will come naturally to you. The sensations in your brain become light and beautiful. These are the experiences you can obtain when the prāṇa is awakened.

Question: Is yoga good for people at any age?

Answer: According to tradition, there are 840,000 postures. Out of the 840,000 postures there are 84 main postures with about three hundred variations. In these variations you will find the appropriate exercises for every age group and every condition of the body. Sick people, elderly people, young people, children, people of every walk of life can find appropriate postures to begin their practice. As they practice, they will be able to expand to a greater variety of postures.

Question: Do you have any anecdotes or stories of famous people who have taken up yoga?

Answer: There are many people. Amongst them are the Beatles. It was in 1964 or 1965. I used to give lectures and classes for people who were spending the winter in Nassau, Bahamas. They would arrange a hall free of charge for this activity. But on that day the hall was not available, because the next day it was going to be used by the Beatles for a performance. The Beatles had come to Nassau to shoot a film called "Help!".

That night I called my host and asked him to please change my programme to another day. I felt that I should meet the Beatles, I felt that they had some connection with yoga. I went to see them in person with four copies of my *Complete Illustrated Book of Yoga*. When I came to the hall they were not there. They were shooting the film at the Nassau airport.

When I came to the location, the director informed the Beatles that a swami wanted to give some books to them. They were moving around like children, playing and bicycling. All four came to meet me. I autographed the books and presented them. When Ringo opened the book and saw the headstand, he said "My God, I can't even stand on my feet. How I am I going to be able to stand on my head?" But George asked some serious questions about yoga. I knew that he would be instrumental to bring the message of yoga to the young people; many in this generation at that time had not enough control over their thinking. So, in a way I introduced yoga through them and that helped.

Another person is the late Peter Sellers. He was with me for my peace mission. The last time I saw him was in Dublin. Unfortunately, he is not here anymore on this earth plane. He was a good Yogi. He kept his regular routine and used to practice meditation, āsanas, and prāṇāyāma. I gave him the spiritual name Atmarama; he once gave me a Pink Panther card, where he signed with his spiritual name Atmaram.

I saw many other people who all took up yoga and made other people also realize the value of yoga. Through Peter Sellers, many movie stars and other people started practicing yoga.

Question: Can you define exactly why people should start practicing yoga?

Answer: There are five aspects to yoga. You take the human body as a car and this car, the human body, also needs five things just like in a motor car. Whether you bought the latest model of Rolls-Royce or an ordinary Volkswagen Beetle, every car needs five things. First, it needs oil and lubrication, second it needs a battery, third it needs a cooling system, fourth it needs the right kind of fuel, and fifth a sensible driver behind the wheel. It doesn't matter which model of car it is; these are the five essential requirements.

This human body is not the soul. The soul uses this body as a vehicle. Five things are essential for this physical vehicle. First oiling and lubrication, it corresponds to the āsanas or postures. In the car there are wheels and gears, in the body you have the joints. The joints are moved by the muscles. Depending on the kind of joint movement they create, the muscles act as flexors, extensors, abductors, adductors, pronators, supinators, elevators, protruders and retractors. Any muscle can only do one thing. It can pull, it cannot push. Muscles are arranged in opposite places: for example, if I contract my biceps this bends the elbow, and the opposite muscle is stretched. When I extend my elbow the triceps contracts and the bicep stretches. This is called opposite bi-alignment. If there is tightness in one section, it brings immobility in the joint. Suppose your triceps is too tight. Then when the bicep tries to contract, it will result in considerably reduced mobility.

For most of us it is in the forward bending that many of our muscles are shortened. We cannot stretch well, and this creates typical problems in the back, along the spine and in other joints. Yogis try to correct this improper bodily alignment through āsanas or postures. This corresponds to oiling and lubricating the motor.

Also, all exercise is meant to increase circulation and keep the blood vessels flexible and increase the oxygen levels. In other exercises like jogging or running, deep breathing does occur, but there is always some oxygen deficit due to the intense muscle work. This oxygen debt or increase of carbon dioxide leads to formation of lactic acid, which causes muscle fatigue. In yogic exercise this fatigue is avoided through proper breathing. At the same time the blood vessels are kept flexible, and the circulation increases. It is due to non-vegetarian diet that the cholesterol calcium-like deposits slowly accumulate in the arteries. This hardens and narrows the arteries, finally leading to blockage of the blood circulation.

If this happens in the coronary arteries of the heart, one may get a heart attack; when it happens in the brain one may get a stroke. High blood pressure and heart problems are a major health problem of the West because the food intake is much too high in protein. This is also a problem for the liver. Too much intake of protein creates deposits in the joints, forming arthritis; the buildup of uric acid in turn creates high cholesterol levels and hardening of the arteries. It is a disaster for both the heart and the circulatory system, including the brain.

Yogic exercise along with proper diet keep the arteries flexible which then can expand and contract easily each time when the heart pumps. This creates a smooth flow of blood. In hardened arteries the blood flow goes in spurts because the walls of the arteries cannot expand. Yogic exercises keep the arteries flexible: as you can see in the pictures of our new book, each movement like forward or backward bending, pulls the muscles along with the blood vessels and helps to keep the circulation level up. Also, the breathing is done in such a way that we never create an oxygen debt. If during exercise you breathe deeper than normal there will be no oxygen deficiency at all. Thus, there will be no muscle fatigue.

Yoga exercises are not merely physical exercise but include breathing, diet and mind control. All three come together.

So, the first point is proper exercise or āsanas which are like oiling and lubricating the motor.

The second point is proper breathing. Just as a car needs a charged battery, the body needs to recharge the solar plexus. Prāṇāyāma recharges our solar plexus.

The third point is proper relaxation. In between the āsanas there is relaxation. Yoga is not merely exercising. Relaxation is as important as exercise, but it will not come naturally. If I contract my muscles, I must also know how to relax my muscles. I must give them a command. So, the mind plays an important part.

Besides the supply of oxygen and prāṇa, the body also needs energy through proper diet, the proper kind of gas or fuel. As a fourth point, yoga recommends a vegetarian diet.

And the fifth point is a sensible driver behind the wheel which is the mind. The mind controls the body. When we can control the body through positive thinking and meditation, then we will have complete holistic health.

This is why yoga is important. It is not only treating one aspect and neglecting the others. Many people practice exercise and develop their muscles, but they forget to develop the internal organs. Others only practice meditation but do not do anything with their body. Others only just do running and exercise but their diet is horrible and they even smoke.

This is why yoga is essential. What is also unique is that for yoga you do not need a big space. You can do in your living room or in the bedroom. The postures are easy to practice, and your family members can join you. Father, mother, children, all can practice these five points without having any difficulty.

Question: Does it matter to which religion you belong if you want to practice yoga? Suppose I'm a Christian or Muslim, is it going to conflict with my beliefs at all?

Answer: Anybody can practice yoga. Whether you are Christian or Muslim, everybody must breathe, and so do you. Therefore, all will benefit from learning to breathe properly through prāṇāyāma breathing exercises. Whether Christian, Muslim, Jewish or Hindu, everybody will get arthritis if they eat a meat diet. It can be prevented by the right diet which yoga teaches.

Yoga gives peace of mind through meditation techniques. Meditation teaches how to stop the mind. This can be practiced by gazing at a flower, at a candle, at a cross, at the star of David, or a picture of Kṛṣṇa or Rāma, or Om, or a black dot, or at a star. The image which is used may differ, but the technique to control the mind is the same.

Just like heat is necessary for cooking, no matter what type of dish is being prepared. Heat can come from ordinary firewood or cow dung like in India, or from gas, or from an electric stove, but there will always be heat. Similarly in meditation, the fundamental technique is the same, there is no separation at all. Meditation always consists of stilling or calming the mind: *"yoga's-citta-vṛtti-nirodhaḥ"* – "yoga is stilling the thought waves of the mind", so that we can find peace. To still the mind, an object or a point must be given to the mind to focus upon. The focal point can be a cakra like the ājñā cakra or the viśuddha cakra or any other internal plexus; this kind of concentration object is not connected to any religion. It can also be an external object, or a picture of any deity or holy symbol such as the crescent moon of the Muslim religion. The object can differ, but the technique is the same. The believers of any religion can practice meditation.

There are also many types of mantras. Some of them are connected to Kṛṣṇa, but there are also mantras like aiṃ, hrīm, klīm, etcetera which do not have any specific meaning. It is just the pronunciation of a spiritual sound which only has a mystical meaning. It is characterized by an energy pattern on which you concentrate, and which then also changes the vibrations of your body.

Everybody practices yoga and meditation either knowingly or unknowingly. When you fast, it is yoga. And when you go and pray and concentrate on an altar that's called meditation. That's also yoga. Or when you just think of philosophy, a philosophical life is also a part of yoga. When you do service of humanity that's called karma yoga. When you go to church and worship God, that devotional practice is called bhakti yoga. In fact, everyone is practicing yoga whether they know it or not, whether they name it or not.

Question: What are the origins of yoga? Where did it come from? How did it start?

Answer: The oldest science of life started in the Himalayas. These great masters wanted to find out two things: How to get out of pain and how to conquer death? We are all looking at these two problems. Everyone has some form of pain and we all must leave this planet earth one day. In their search of an answer to these questions, these masters discovered that there is no death for the Self. Death is only for this body. It is inevitable. Everything is changing. Our body is not different from this flower – both are changing moment by moment. My grey hair did not come all at once, the color changed moment by moment. Even now it is changing but I cannot see it. Thousands and thousands of cells in my body are dying this very moment but I am not aware of it. This universe is constantly changing but the Self, the subject does not change. Through meditation we can find this subject, what we call Self, Atman, Soul or God. When we have found that, then and only then will we be able to remove pain and suffering. This is how all yoga started.

To reach this painless, immortal state you have to transcend the various bodies or vehicles, the physical, the astral and the causal bodies. The physical pain of the physical body can be transcended through the practice of āsanas. Through prāṇāyāma you can control emotional pain and so on. Through different techniques, different types of pain are transcended, one can realize the immortal Self.

Question: Is it attachment that causes the pain in the first place?

Answer: Yes, the attachment to objects. Suppose I am attached to this glass because it has been used by King George X. I bought it in an auction for a very high price. Now it is mine. I am so much attached to the glass that I won't give it to anybody, I protect it. But you are also interested to have the glass and somehow you manage to take it from me. Now it is yours, I cannot call it mine anymore.

Unfortunately, the glass slips from your hand, falls to the ground, and breaks. I laugh and you are crying. This is how attachment works. The object is there. If it would have fallen to the ground when it belonged to me, it would have broken my heart. But now that it's not mine but yours, there is no pain for me. Thus, it is not the object, but the attachment to objects that brings pain. When you go to the Self, you see that there is nothing you can own. Everything belongs to God and you are everything. At that time there is no pain.

Question: What is the purpose of meditation?

Answer: The aim of meditation consists of transcending the attachments and the hypnotic state in which we presently are. The idea that I am a Catholic, a Protestant, a Jew, an Arab, a Hindu, that I am tall, black, British, American, or Argentinian. We must escape from this hypnotic state. We are not Israeli, we are not Argentinian, we are not tall, we are not short.

Suppose an Arab mother and a Jewish mother deliver their baby at the same time in the same hospital. But there is an explosion and confusion, and the babies are given to the wrong mothers. The Arab baby is handed over to the Jewish mother and vice versa. They take their baby home without knowing that their baby has been exchanged. Now the Arab mother loves her Jewish baby just like her own and vice versa. But when they grow up, the Arab child of the Jewish family must fight Arab people and the Jewish child of the Arab family must fight his own Jewish people.

The identification with these names and forms, with these qualifications is not real. We do not have a real understanding of who we are.

Because your parents told you that you are English,

Jewish, Catholic or Protestant, you then start believing that. Meditation is the only answer to escape from this deep hypnotic state. Meditation brings the understanding that I am not this body. I am not Catholic. I am not Protestant. I am not Hindu. I am That I am. "I and my Father are one". That is what Jesus said. That I is in you and that I is in me. We are one.

That is the purpose of meditation. It creates oneness. The Bible describes it as "the peace that passes all understanding". We are all looking for that peace or happiness. It is not outside, it is within. Until we go into meditation and find that inner peace there will be no peace outside.

Question: Can you tell us how the mind works and explain the meaning of manas, buddhi, chitta and ahaṅkara?

Answer: According to the Indian system the mind has four functions. Manas or thinking, buddhi or intellect, citta or subconscious and ahaṅkara or ego. All these different aspects are part of the same mind. The mind uses all these aspects to come to a conclusion. For example, I am seeing something white nearby.

First manas asks the question what is it? Is it paper, is it plastic? Is it a flower? Next the intellect or buddhi says: okay, I will find this out for you. Then the intellect connects with chitta or the subconscious mind to look for the data. The white object is soft, so it could be a flower petal. It could also be a piece of soft silk cloth. The next comparison is with smell. Yes, it smells like something which I know from a previous experience combined with that white color. It is not plastic, and it smells like a flower. After comparing all the data, the intellect concludes: yes, it is a flower petal. It is not plastic; it is not silk. The intellect is the instrument which finds out that it is a flower petal. Finally, the ego asserts: I know it is a flower petal.

Thinking and doubting is called Manas. The intellect is called buddhi and the subconscious mind is called citta. And finally, the ahaṅkara or ego affirms: I know or I do not know. These four processes are stopped in meditation. This leads to ultimate knowledge or transcendental experience.

The mind is very difficult to control. Patanjali says, *"yoga's-citta-vṛtti-nirodhaḥ"*. "Yoga occurs when the oscillation of thought waves coming from the mind is stopped." Like the waves in the ocean. There is no difference between the ocean and the waves. They are all made up of the same water but when that water takes a particular shape, then you call it a wave and see it as different from the background, which is the ocean. Each wave has a particular form, height, velocity and so on. Similarly, our mind is like the ocean with constant movement of various types of thought waves. Sometimes thoughts are positive, sometimes they are negative, sometimes neutral, sometimes there are very passionate thoughts, sometimes the thoughts are very angry, sometimes they are mild. Certain waves are like a small ripple, sometimes the thoughts are like tidal waves. This constant arising of thoughts disturbs our peace. Yoga teaches meditation so you can stop the thought process. Peace arises in a calm mind.

The mind is a very long subject, so we can only mention some aspects here. There are three levels of the mind: the subconscious mind, the conscious mind, and the superconscious mind. The subconscious mind is the built-in instinct, the conscious mind is where reasoning and conclusions happen. Most people function with these two processes, instinct, and intellect. Very few people have intuition. Intuition is often confused with instinct. Instinct is not the same than intuition. Intuition is universal peace and love and accessible through the practice of meditation. Though we do possess intuition, it is not developed. This can be compared with animals who have intellect, but which is not developed. Animals function mostly on the level of instinct. Through meditation we open the channel of intuition where we see oneness and universal consciousness.

Question: Can you tell us a little about advaita vedānta.

Answer: The purpose is to find the Self. The body is just like this cloth, it is an object. It is my cloth, but I am not the cloth. I can give this cloth to you, and I can take it back. This flower is also an object. I can give it to you, or I can take it back. This finger is also an object. I can cut it and give it to you. Then you will have eleven fingers and I only have nine fingers. But the fact that I have taken one finger off, the subject "I am" is still the same. The "I" did not change. Suppose my heart is not functioning, now I can get a monkey heart. Yet I am still the same person, the "I am", the subject and its state do not change. Maybe soon afterwards I need to have a pig liver. In fact, one man had a pig liver. Next, I will receive goat kidneys. A little bit later I need complete blood transfusion. Now all my Hindu blood has been changed into British blood. Finally, I need plastic surgery and I will now have a plastic nose. So, with a monkey heart, pig liver, goat kidneys, British blood and a plastic nose: who am I? The subject always remains the same.

Vedanta says that change is only in the objects. From the body to all the galaxies – these are all objects. They are changing. They will change and no one can stop this. Yet the subject, the Atman or the soul remain eternally the same. Immortality lies in the consciousness of the subject – "I am that I am". I and my Father are one. That Self, Father or God are one and the same. That's called Vedanta. Aham Brahmā Asmi or I am the Absolute. In the saying of Jesus, I is Aham and Father is brahmān. Brahmān and the I or the subject are one and the same. That is called Vedanta.

That subject is not far away, that God is also in you, and you are in me. We are not different, we are one. Vedanta leads to oneness, universal love, universal consciousness. Only by that message will we be able to avoid war and bring peace in this world.

Question: You speak about yoga as a science. How does it compare with other sciences?

Answer: In the Indian system, religion, hygiene, and science are not seen as separate, they are all parts of the same system. In general, what is called science consists of observing certain things through the senses. But when you observe this flower, tell me, can you see any change taking place in this flower?

Interviewer: No.

Swami Vishnudevananda: But is it taking place?

Interviewer: Yes.

Swami Vishnudevananda: It is slowly getting withered, but you cannot see it. Only after some days can you see the change. But how do you know it is changing? You know it through reasoning. Right now, my body is changing, even though I do not see it. But I know it through reasoning, because fifty years ago my body was not like that. Not everything can be experienced through science. Changes which take place moment by moment cannot be experienced, because we cannot measure the present moment. The present moment is when the future changes into the past. The measurement of the present moment is unimaginable, we cannot measure the present moment. Before we can measure it, it has gone into the past. The past is gone forever, and the future is not happening yet. The very moment the future comes into the present, it has already gone into the past. Time cannot be measured, yet we know there is a time.

So, we establish a measurement for time, with the ticking of a clock, and we call this a second. Even though the present moment cannot be measured, science says we can measure one thousandth of a second. Still the question remains, how many thousandths of a second make one moment? No one can say.

From the yogic point of view there are two types of science. Objective knowledge, called jñāna vṛtti, and subjective knowledge, called jñāna svarūpa. The knowledge which we obtain of the outside world through science is temporary. We cannot get the absolute truth of an object by scientific method. The experience of the scientific truth is momentary, and it will change once you apply a different method of observation. If I observe it through a microscope, the experience of the object will be different from looking at it directly with the eyes. If the object is experienced through a most sophisticated instrument in the future, we may just see an energy pattern, which is not visible to the naked eye. Science provides an experience at a particular moment which is sufficient for our intellect. Quantum physics gives scientific evidence of the limitation of objective observation.

Newton sat under the tree, and saw an apple fall to the ground. He asked the question, why did the apple fall? There must be gravity. He discovered gravity. When Einstein symbolically sat under the same tree, he thought: did the apple really come down or did the tree go up and therefore the apple touched the ground? The theory of relativity came. Who is right?

In the sixteenth century Copernicus said that the earth is the center, and that the sun is going around the earth. Then Galileo said it is not possible that the sun is moving. The sun is the center, the earth is going around the sun. Naturally he was persecuted. And with time so many new discoveries have come up.

Science is constantly adjusting its views. At one point it was believed that the atom cannot be broken. Then it was discovered that the atom can be split. Then it was said that there is nothing beyond electrons and protons and neutrons, and that this is the end of the matter. But now it is said that one can also go beyond that, that there are many other subatomic particles. Science cannot tell what the absolute matter is and where matter ends.

Scientific investigation refers to a scientific value given at a particular moment from a particular perspective. Metaphysics is also gaining knowledge, but it does not claim to have the ultimate truth.

Whatever you learn and understand is made of duality and duality will change all the time. The Science of Self is the ultimate science because it relates to that which does not change.

In yoga we look at objective science and subjective science. Āsana and prāṇāyāma are objective science, they refer to the body. But the subjective science of the Self does not belong to any known science. In the knowledge of "I am That I am" no ordinary mental function takes place.

Science is only a word which we are using. I can investigate into the benefits of an āsana and conclude it is good for such and such health purpose. Or controlling the mind through a particular meditation brings a particular peaceful experience. It gives a value, but that doesn't mean the value is permanent. It is relative.

At one moment we find that a particular invention is good. But sometimes later it is seen that it is bringing some reactions and it is taken off the market. Today it is good, and tomorrow is not good. Science is not an absolute truth.

Question: What are the four paths of yoga and why have you chosen to teach rāja yoga more than the others?

Answer: The four paths of yoga are not antagonistic to each other or independently divided into compartments. There are four types of minds: some are very emotional, others are more active, others are mystical or scientific in approach, and others are of an intellectual type.

For example, if someone receives a flower. An emotional person will say "Oh, thank you" and see the wonderful beauty of the flower and connect to it with love and emotion: "Someone loves me". If you are an active, artistic person, you may immediately try to make a drawing of the flower. If you are scientifically minded, your reaction may be: What is the nature of the flower? To which botanical group does it belong? And an intellectual philosopher may think: "This beauty is temporary. By tomorrow the flower will have withered and lie on the floor. People may then just walk over its beauty. This beauty is not permanent. Its beauty is only temporary. It's fooling me but I won't be caught." In this way the same object will create different types of experience depending on the type of mind.

Therefore, when we try to explain the yogic techniques of mind control to a person of an emotional temperament, you cannot just give the same message to other types of people who are intellectual, active, mystic, or scientific.

What type of method are you going to suggest to an emotional person? It would be bhakti yoga, which changes or sublimates the energy of emotion into devotion.

Other people are very active like politicians and business-people, they cannot sit and meditate on mantras, or go to churches. For them the message is to see God in all and see work as service. Service is Karma yoga. It is a long subject; this is just to give you an idea.

The temperament of the rāja yoga approach is more scientific: it moves step by step, just like a scientist would proceed. You practice āsanas and see the benefits. As you progress you can see changes in the energy flow. But the goal is to go beyond the intellectual understanding, beyond the step-by-step experience and reach the transcendental state.

Jnana yoga is philosophical. It analyses: this body is made of atoms, it is made of food, so it must go back to food. Therefore, the I cannot be the body. So, who am I really? Where did I come from? Where will I go?

The four approaches are not antagonistic to each other, they are not four separate compartments. An intellectual person has also some emotion. He is also active, and he also has a scientific nature. In the same way an emotional person has also other qualities.

It is advised to use one yoga as a main practice and add the other approaches as an auxiliary practice.

I took to haṭha yoga because it is more scientific. That is my nature. But that does not mean that I am only interested in the scientific approach. I also know about vedanta philosophy, and I am also interested in karma yoga or service.

Therefore, I started a peace mission, trying to bring peace to humanity; that is my karma yoga. I also go to worship and perform devotional practices like āratī. All aspects of yoga blend together, they are not independent.

Question: Can you tell us about karma? How does it work?

Answer: Karma literally means action. This implies both action and reaction. Ultimately, karma also means destiny and fate.

Your present life, what you see now, must have a cause. This beautiful flower came into existence from a bulb. From this bulb came the actual manifestation. There is cause and effect, action and reaction. Or if I take a ball and throw it against the wall, it bounces back. Depending on the action of throwing, the ball bounces back with a similar force. There is a law of physics which says that every action has an opposite and equal reaction. This corresponds to the law of karma.

If you perform a good action or a bad action, there will be a corresponding reaction. You cannot stop this. It is an energy, and that energy must fulfill a specific purpose, it becomes destiny. The action which you are performing now will become the destiny of tomorrow. If you plant a seed today, after three years you will get the fruit, either an apple or an orange according to the seed you sowed. If you sow a bitter seed, you'll get a bitter fruit, if you sow a sweet seed, you will get a sweet orange. All that is karma or destiny.

Our present life is the result of past action. Past actions have brought you to a particular place with its nature or condition. The actions which we are performing now will change our life in the future. Some people are happy. It is not God who made them happy. Some people are poor. It is not God who made them poor. God is impartial. It is due to actions which we have sown in the past and which are now returning and materializing.

We have a Yoga Retreat and a Yoga Camp and so many people have come. I never had the faintest idea of this in my mind. I founded these places and people came. The staff and yogis in the centers are working as volunteers. Why are they working without a pay? Because their action from the past was to serve. They have the same service mentality now. It gives them a type of peace.

Karma is action and reaction, commonly called destiny. A person's life is caused by past action, and present action is creating future destiny.

In conclusion, yoga starts with the body but never stops with the body. The body is a means. To achieve anything, you need a healthy body. Take care of the body through the five principles of yoga. If you do not take care of the body, if you try to suppress a disease, it will affect you physically and emotionally.

It is like driving a car and suddenly there appears a red light on the dashboard. It indicates that the oil pressure is low. Then another red light goes on informing that the cooling system is not working, the engine is getting hot. A third light says that the battery is not charging, and a fourth light shows that there is not enough gas or petrol in the tank.

But I am a good mechanic. I can stop all the problems. I open my glove compartment and take out a hammer and break all the red lights. And then I start driving the car!

This is happening also in our body. Doctors give prescription drugs: if you have a headache, kill the pain. If you have arthritis, kill the pain. If you have a heart problem, kill the pain. Pain killers do not solve any of these problems. It is like breaking the red lights on the dashboard. Pain is the only language of the body to inform us that something is wrong.

Yoga advises that the moment you have any problem, begin to fast, and put the body into a relaxed and restful state. The moment you fast, the metabolic activity in the body slows down. The heart, liver, spleen, kidneys, pancreas, all the organs reduce their function. Then the body has time to readjust and recuperate the energy or prāṇa to remove the problem. Through fasting and a little bit of breathing, āsana and meditation you can remove almost any sickness. But when you try to suppress the symptoms of a disease through pain pills etc, you are just breaking the red lights. You are not removing the cause.

Yoga is not a theory; you must put it into practice. Then you will experience the benefits. If you want to know the taste of honey, no amount of talking about honey can make you understand. Only once you put a small amount of honey into your mouth, you will say "Oh this is honey. This is sweet." Put it into practice, you will yourself see the benefits.

LECTURE EXCERPTS FROM THE 1952/1953 ALL INDIA TOUR

In July of 1952, Swami Sivananda sent Swami Vishnudevananda on a 12-month tour throughout India, during which he taught and lectured in 50 cities. The Sivananda Ashram in Rishikesh published a summary of his tour.

"Sri Swami Vishnudevananda is one of those rare God-intoxicated souls who often forget their body and environments and delight in blissful communion with the Self in silence and solitude. Though he is an advanced adept in haṭha yoga, he has unequalled faith in God and guru, he is a great bhakta and a dynamic karma yogi, too. He is humble, simple, and pure, God-like in his wisdom and child-like in his nature.

Hundreds of spiritual aspirants all over India who, thrilled by the hair-raising demonstration of yoga āsanas and kriyas (cleansing exercises) and illuminating lectures on the various paths to God, by Sri Swami Vishnudevananda during his All India Tour asked that a summary of the lectures be published. We are confident that Swami's lectures would be of great use to all sādhakas (seekers)."

Left: Swami Vishnudevananda demonstrates the scorpion asana in front of Swami Sivananda

Benefits of Yoga

Āsanas and prāṇāyāma are part of yoga sādhana. They can confer their spiritual benefits upon you only if they are based on the foundations of yama-niyama , a strong character; and if they get the help of auxiliaries like a sattwic (pure) diet and daily life. Otherwise, they will be merely physical exercises. Of course, you will enjoy good health and freedom from disease. But, of what use is health and strength, if the mind within is rotting, and the canker of evil is eating into your very vitals?

I would emphasize here that the practice of āsanas and prāṇāyāma tends to conserve the prāṇa, makes the prāṇa flow in, and harmonizes your entire system. As they eradicate tamas (inertia) and rajas (agitation), sattwa (purity) grows in you. Supplement this by taking a sattwic diet, by leading a sattwic life. Do not take any food or drink that agitates the nerves. You will then experience a marvelous change in your mind. You will ever be calm, peaceful, and blissful.

True it is that the practice of āsanas and prāṇāyāma, combined with the intake of sattwic diet automatically gives you a sattwic mind, shuts out all impure thoughts and desires and promotes sublime thoughts and aspirations in your mind. But, in the beginning stages, when this effect has not been full achieved, you should make positive efforts, too, to achieve this result. How can you fill a pot even if you pour millions of gallons into it, if there is a big hole at its bottom?

So, you can readily understand that if you want to derive the maximum benefit from your practice, you should keep the mind pure and lead a harmonious outward life so that the body may be able to receive and profit by the abundant inflow of pranic energy. The reward is great and worth the little discipline that we impose upon ourselves.

Haṭha Yoga is not only Physical

For an external observer, haṭha yoga appears to be an entirely physical process. Many people nowadays do āsanas and prāṇāyāma merely for maintaining good health and correcting certain defects of the functioning of the body. No doubt, haṭha yoga enables you to maintain perfect health. And, in this respect haṭha yoga is infinitely superior to all kinds of physical culture and infinitely superior to all tonics and medicines; for it enables you to tap the infinite source of vital power lying latent within you.

But haṭha yoga is much more than all this. It is a spiritual practice and, in this respect, ranks on a par with vedantic meditation, the practice of the highest form of devotion to God, or egoless service of the Lord in all (karma yoga). This is the most essential point I pray that all bear in mind. Haṭha yoga is a most scientific method of controlling the mind. Mind has its vibrant power in the prāṇa, so to say, and it flows to the various organs.

As yoga restrains the prāṇa, automatically the activities of the mind are curbed. The organs of perception and action are animated by prāṇa; their play also is restricted by prāṇāyāma. Thus, you get perfect control of body and mind very easily through the practice of āsanas and prāṇāyāma. Practice haṭha yoga. Within a very short time, you will know its benefits. You will enjoy a peace of mind and an inward bliss that you cannot get from any external source. You will have great control over emotions. Lust, anger, jealousy, and other baser passions will vanish. You will have greater will power.

Recharge the Inner Battery

Modern life is one long expenditure of vital energy. Eating, drinking, working, speaking – everything involves expenditure of the life-force. When is man regaining that force? Lack of brahmacarya (control of sexual energy) is another great drain on the vital force. You can recharge this inner battery of life-force through the practice of āsanas, prāṇāyāma, and meditation.

Āsanas involve some control of breath or life energy. Prāṇāyāma develops the life energy through breath retention. Meditation puts you in touch with the supreme reservoir of power and life. Therefore, everyone should regularly practice these yogic disciplines and constantly recharge the inner battery. This is the way to enjoy health and long life.

From the Gross to the Subtle

Swami Sivananda has emphasized again and again that haṭha yoga should invariably form part of the integral sādhana of every aspirant. Many people ignore this as a mere set of physical feats unnecessary for yoga sādhana, and sometimes a hindrance, too. That is because, they have not yet understood the link between the gross and subtle.

You all know that Vedanta teaches that there are five kośas enveloping the Self: annamaya, prāṇamaya, manomaya, vijñānamaya and ānandamaya kośas. Each kośa interpenetrates the other. Annamaya is gross; prāṇamaya is subtler. Manomaya is still subtler. In a subtle manner prāṇamaya kośa interpenetrates the annamaya kośa. Each cell of the body vibrates with prāṇa. In the body there are 72,000 nāḍis or pranioelectric wires that carry this pranic current to every individual cell of the body. Now, you can visualize that even if you forget this gross physical body, you have within you its complete "double" in the shape of this electric pranic body. Similar is the case of manomaya kośa, which interpenetrates this prāṇamaya kośa.

Only now is the aspirant ready for the deeper inner sādhana (spiritual practice) of pratyāhāra (withdrawal of the senses), dhāraṇa (concentration) and dhyāna (meditation), that lead him to samādhi (superconscious state). When the nāḍis (subtle energy channels) are impure and clogged here and there, when the prāṇa vibrates inharmoniously through them, there mind will either be dull (tamasic) or restless (rajasic).

The greater time and attention the aspirant devotes to the initial preliminaries, the quicker and surer will he attain siddhi (mastery) in his higher yoga practices. Yama and Niyama should therefore receive our greatest attention. They are the foundations, as it were, to the whole edifice of yoga. They are the first two steps in rāja yoga. If one is established in Yama (ahiṁsā, satya, brahmacarya, asteya and aparigraha), and in the practice of Niyama (sauca, santoṣa, tapas, svādhyāya and Īśvara praṇidhāna:), then and only then will it be possible for him to make any progress in yoga at all.

Then come āsana and prāṇāyāma as the third and fourth limbs of the external rāja yoga but which, as you can well understand, have a tremendous influence on the internal personality of man. Then comes the purely internal practice of Pratyāhāra or the withdrawal of the senses from their outgoing tendencies. The sādhaka is dead to the world, but very much alive within himself. Then dhāraṇa (concentration): he fixes his mind on the lakshya (goal) within, on the Lord within, on his own Self. Dhyāna (meditation) which naturally follows automatically leads to samādhi by long, continued practice.

Even in these higher, inner yoga practices, haṭha yogis believe that it is when through the protracted practice of prāṇāyāma, when the prāṇa enters the suṣumṇa (central canal), that the aspirant gets pratyāhāra, and a prolongation of this state is termed by them as dhāraṇa, dhyāna and samādhi. For the prāṇa that has entered the suṣumṇa and which is totally prevented from flowing out, does not stand still, but rapidly progresses along the suṣumṇa, taking the kuṇḍalinī śakti form cakra to cakra till She attains Union with Śiva in the sahasrāra. This is when the yogi enjoys the bliss of samādhi.

That is the aim of haṭha yoga. Āsanas and prāṇāyāma have blissful samādhi as their goal. Forget not this fact. They are essentially spiritual practices. They ensure your physical and mental well-being. They free you from diseases, weakness, and inertia. They impart luster to your whole body and invigorate the entire system is an added glory to the Yogic system, their goal is something much higher.

Life without Meditation is a Waste

No one who has not practiced concentration and meditation can really appreciate what a great loss he is suffering. If you taste the bliss of meditation even for a day, you will think that a life without meditation is a waste of life. In your daily life, you let this wonderful divine power, which is within you, the power of consciousness, which is reflected in your mind, flow out and illumine various perishable objects of the world. All the pleasure that you get from the worldly objects is the pleasure that is inherent in this consciousness! Yet delusion makes us feel that we derive pleasure from objects. Thus, this waste of consciousness and power goes on unhindered. You feel it is natural to think all sorts of thoughts, to do this and that, to spend your mental energy on useless things.

One day if you shut out all thoughts, if you redirect all the rays of the mind back on itself, if you rest in your own Self – then will you know what a fountain of power and bliss are within you. Then will you yearn for more and more of this. Then will you feel that even a moment spent in letting this consciousness flow outward is pain and pain alone. Concentration is not so easy; from time immemorial we have been accustomed to letting the mind roam in outside objects. Long, continued practice is necessary. Real vairāgya (non-attachment) born of discrimination is necessary. Then āsana and prāṇāyāma will help you.

Practice concentration in brahmāmuhurtha (4:00 am). It will be easier for you to collect the rays of the mind and concentrate on the Self within. Sit in padmāsana (lotus pose) or siddhāsana (adept's pose) in a secluded place. Pray to the Lord and to your guru to bless you. Do Japa (mantra repetition). Japa is the staff on which you can safely lean as you enter the realm of concentration. The breath will become rhythmic and calm.

You can wonderfully combine japa and prāṇāyāma. When the breath is restrained, when the thought-waves subside, then the name of the Lord will begin to glow within you with radiance and life. You will be conscious of nothing else. Go on and on with japa till the mind is perfectly concentrated. Cling to the lotus feet of the Lord. If evil thoughts arise in the mind, ignore them; do not identify yourself with them; do not wrestle with them. Cling ever more firmly to the lotus feet of the Lord. They will pass away. Concentration will then deepen into meditation, and you will feel the divinity within you in all Its glory. Then samādhi will follow and you will realize God.

Even in your daily life in the world, your heart will constantly yearn to experience the joy of God-consciousness. You can yourself positively cultivate this in the early stages of your sādhana, by selfless service with ātma-bhāv (seeing the presence of the Self) and nārāyanā-bhāv (seeing the Lord in all). Serve all. Serve the sick, the suffering, the destitute. See not the names and forms, but the indwelling supreme presence. This will hasten your progress in concentration and meditation; and the latter will help you see the Lord in all. Thus, you will understand that service and realization are the two wings of the same bird of Self-knowledge.

This is the supreme teaching of Gurudev. This is divine life. This is the great path to the summit of divine glory which Gurudev has opened for us. May we all tread this path and attain the summum bonum of life.

The Nature of Swami Sivananda

Gurudev is all to everybody. Everyone who approaches Gurudev feels that he is their all, father, mother, friend, god and child. Like the fond mother, he offers warm and loving security in his omnipotent arms, security from the onslaughts of māyā, security from the dangers and pitfalls that lie on the path of the sādhaka. This love can only be compared to the mother's love for her new-born babe. I would be saying very little when I say that he has sacrificed his all in order that we may evolve. Just as the mother has but the one thought of the child's welfare, he has only one thought – the thought of our spiritual progress.

When, on our path, we stumble and fall, he lovingly lifts us up. He does not scold us or find fault with us as an unwise father does. But he sympathizes with us, he gives us new hope, fresh encouragement, and infinite consolation, –

as every wise father should do. He asks us to brace ourselves up and plod on.

But do not for a moment think that Swamiji is all butter and honey, all soft as a rose. When we kneel before him in utter humility, when we approach him as we approach God, when we crave for the higher things of life, – he instantly appears to us as God Himself, in all his unspeakable majesty, awe-inspiring grandeur. From his high throne of Self-realization he blesses us, enlightens us.

If Gurudev were all the time so high and beyond our reach, we would all be held at a distance. We would not follow him. We would look upon him as a super-divine being, to be kept aloof and worshipped. In the twinkling of an eye, he transforms himself into our very dear friend. This sage, this god, this embodiment of the Supreme Being, plays with us, cuts jokes with us, makes us laugh merrily and laughs himself, listens to us as though we are wiser than him, asks for advice as though he is perplexed. In an instant we find that we are close to him at heart. We are drawn to him. We are conquered. He conquers us so that we might conquer ourselves and attain union with the Self.

Treat him as your own. Feel that he is yours. He is your child. He is completely child-like, simple, artless, godly. Thus is he, the great sage of the Himalayas. But I may sing his glories before you for centuries; all that would not enable you to understand him truly, as he is in actual life at the Ashram, in his own divine presence, within his divine aura.

The Voice of the Himalayas

Time and again, great avatāras (incarnations) of the Lord like Lord Kṛṣṇa, and so many saints and sages who are enlightened with perfect wisdom, come into our midst to awaken us, and to lead us along the path of divine life to the goal of divine light. The voice of Śrī Kṛṣṇa, the voice of the *Bhagavad Gītā,* is heard even today as the voice of the Himalayas. It is the voice of my Gurudev Sri Swami Sivanandaji Maharaj.

They all speak with one voice; their message is fundamentally the same. Only the presentation may differ to suit our need, our temperament, and our receptive capacity. What Lord Kṛṣṇa taught thousands of years ago, Swami Sivananda places before us through his every-day life and his words that are crystal clear to us.

This voice of the Himalayas awakens us to the reality of God. Who created this universe? Surely not you or I. By whose power is it maintained? Surely not yours or mine. If all that has been created progresses towards something, moves towards something, towards whom does it all proceed? That supreme something is God. Why do we not reach It, if we are moving towards it from time immemorial? Because, It is within us all! Our search outside for something which is within us is bound to be endless and futile. When we turn our gaze within, then we may find it! The voice of the Himalayas calls us from within, to turn our gaze within, and to recognize the godhead within all.

When we do not recognize that godhead within us, when we are not in contact with that godhead within us, we experience pain, evil and misery. Doubts and difficulties torment us. Vague fears and powerful cravings drive us crazy and mad. When we recognize that godhead and contact that divinity latent in us, we enjoy unbroken peace and infinite bliss. That is what the voice of the Himalayas assures us.

There is some mysterious power which does not allow us to glimpse this reality even for a moment. It veils. It deludes. It presents before us infinite patterns of unreality and makes us feel that that is the reality! It makes us feel there is happiness in the object alone. It makes us feel that only those things which we can experience through our senses are real and that there is nothing beyond. This is māyā. The pleasure-coating we find in this world is māyā. This pleasure does not last. God in His infinite mercy sends us His messengers, the sparks of His grace and love for us. They take the form of misery, pain and evil. They awaken us to the true nature of the world. They awaken us to the truth that we have been vainly searching for eternal bliss in the wrong direction. We should turn our gaze within. The powerful voice of the Himalayas gives us this caution and steals our hearts.

What will a person who is awakened to this truth and who desires to commune with God do? How will a person behave who has completely surrendered himself to the omnipotent will of the Lord? Will he sit idly watching the world? No, says the Lord in the Gita, and His message is illustrated in the life of Swami Sivananda. Such a man would not be a defeatist. His surrender to God will be positive and active. He will, so to say, cooperate with the divine will. He will be filled with God's compassion for His children. He will strive every moment of his life to serve all and love all, and thus to commune with Lord in all, for all time to come. That is the Message of Śrī Kṛṣṇa. And that is the message of my Gurudev, the voice of the Himalayas that is heard throughout the world and that has awakened millions all over the globe.

SIVANANDA YOGA VEDANTA CENTRE ASHRAMS CENTRES

Ashrams

Sivananda Ashram Yoga Camp

673 8th Avenue, Val Morin Québec, J0T 2R0, CANADA
hq@sivananda.org
www.sivananda.org/camp

Sivananda Ashram Yoga Ranch

P.O. Box 195, 500 Budd Road Woodbourne,
NY 12788, UNITED STATES
yogaranch@sivananda.org
www.sivananda.org/ranch

Sivananda Ashram Yoga Retreat

P.O. Box N 7550 Paradise Island, Nassau, BAHAMAS
nassau@sivananda.org
www.sivananda.org/bahamas

Sivananda Yoga Vedanta Dhanwantari Ashram

P.O. Neyyar Dam, Dt. Thiruvananthapuram, Kerala 695 572,
INDIA
guestindia@sivananda.org
www.sivananda.org/neyyardam

Sivananda Ashram Yoga Farm

14651 Ballantree Lane, Comp. 8 Grass Valley, California
CA 95949, UNITED STATES
yogafarm@sivananda.org
www.sivananda.org/farm

Sivananda Yoga Vedanta Meenakshi Ashram

(near Pavana Vilakku Junction) New Natham Road,
Saramthangi Village,
Vellayampatti P.O. Madurai Dt. 625 503, Tamil Nadu, INDIA
madurai@sivananda.org
www.sivananda.org/madurai

Sivananda Kutir (near Siror Bridge)

P.O. Netala, Uttara Kashi District, Uttaranchal, Himalayas
249193, INDIA
himalayas@sivananda.org
www.sivananda.org/netala

Sivananda Yoga Retreat House

Bichlach 40
6370, Reith near Kitzbühel, AUSTRIA
tyrol@sivananda.net
www.sivananda.at

Ashram de Yoga Sivananda

26 impasse du Bignon,
45170 Neuville aux bois, FRANCE
orleans@sivananda.net
sivanandaorleans.org

Sivananda Yoga Vietnam Resort and Training Center

K'Lan Resort,
Hoa Hong Street, Ward 4,
Tuyen Lam Lake
Da Lat City, Lam Dong Province VIETNAM
vietnamyogaresort@sivananda.org
www.sivananda.org/vietnam

Sivananda Yoga Vedanta Tapaswini Ashram

Guthavaripalem, Kadivedu P.O.,
Chilakur Mandalam - 524410, Gudur Nellore DT.,
Andhra Pradesh, INDIA
gudur@sivananda.org
www.sivananda.org/gudur

Centres

AUSTRIA

Sivananda Yoga Vedanta Zentrum

Prinz Eugen Straße 18
Vienna 1040, AUSTRIA
vienna@sivananda.net
wien.sivananda.yoga

CANADA

Sivananda Yoga Vedanta Centre

5178 Saint Laurent Boulevard
Montreal, Quebec, H2T 1R8, CANADA
montreal@sivananda.org
www.sivananda.org/montreal

Sivananda Yoga Vedanta Centre

77 Harbord Street
Toronto, Ontario, M5S 1G4, CANADA
toronto@sivananda.org
https://sivanandacanada.org/toronto/

FRANCE

Centre Sivananda de Yoga Vedanta

140 rue du Faubourg Saint-Martin
75010 Paris, FRANCE
paris@sivananda.net
sivanandaparis.org

GERMANY

Sivananda Yoga Vedanta Zentrum

Luisenstrasse 45
D-80333 Munich, GERMANY
munich@sivananda.net
muenchen.sivananda.yoga

Sivananda Yoga Vedanta Zentrum

Schmiljanstrasse 24
D-12161 Berlin, GERMANY
berlin@sivananda.net
berlin.sivananda.yoga

INDIA

Sivananda Yoga Vedanta Nataraja Centre

A-41 Kailash Colony, New Delhi 110 048, INDIA
delhi@sivananda.org
www.sivananda.org/delhi

Sivananda Yoga Vedanta Dwarka Centre
PSP Pocket, Sector – 6 (near DAV school, next to Kamakshi Apts) Swami Sivananda Marg, Dwarka, New Delhi 110 075, INDIA
dwarka@sivananda.org
www.sivananda.org / dwarka

Sivananda Yoga Vedanta Centre
TC 37 / 1927 (5), Airport Road
West Fort P.O.
695 023 Thiruvananthapuram, Kerala, INDIA
trivandrum@sivananda.org
www.sivananda.org / trivandrum

Sivananda Yoga Vedanta Centre
3 / 655, Kuppam Road, Kaveri Nagar, Kottivakkam, Chennai 600 041,INDIA
chennai@sivananda.org
www.sivananda.org / chennai

Sivananda Yoga Vedanta Centre
444, K.K. Nagar, East 9th Street
625 020 Madurai, Tamil Nadu, INDIA2
maduraicentre@sivananda.org
www.sivananda.org / maduraicentre

ISRAEL

Sivananda Yoga Vedanta Centre
6 Lateris Street, Tel Aviv 64166, ISRAEL
telaviv@sivananda.org
www.sivananda.org / telaviv

JAPAN

Sivananda Yoga Center
Funabashi 4-21-3, Setagaya-ku,
Tokyo, JAPAN,
156-0055
tokyo@sivananda.org
https://sivanandajp.org

Shojiko Retreat
789 Shoji, Fujikawaguchiko-machi,
Minamitsuru-gun, Yamanashi-Ken, JAPAN,
401-0336
shojikoretreat@sivananda.jp
https://sivanandajp.org/shojikoretreat

LITHUANIA

Sivananda Jogos Vedantos Centras
M.K. Čurlionio g. 66
Vilnius 03100, LITUANIA
vilnius@sivananda.net
www.sivananda.lt

SPAIN

Centro de Yoga Sivananda Vedanta
Calle Eraso 4
Madrid 28028, SPAIN
madrid@sivananda.net
www.sivananda.es

SWITZERLAND

Centre Sivananda de Yoga Vedanta

1 rue des Minoteries
Geneva 1205, SWITZERLAND
geneva@sivananda.net
www.sivananda.ch

UNITED KINGDOM

Sivananda Yoga Vedanta Centre

45 – 51 Felsham Road
London SW15 1AZ,
UNITED KINGDOM
london@sivananda.net
sivanandalondon.org

UNITED STATES

Sivananda Yoga Vedanta Center

1246 West Bryn Mawr
Chicago, Illinois 60660,
UNITED STATES
chicago@sivananda.org
www.sivananda.org/chicago

Sivananda Yoga Vedanta Center

243 West 24th Street
New York, NY 10011,
UNITED STATES
newyork@sivananda.org
www.sivananda.org/newyork

Sivananda Yoga Vedanta Center

3741 West 27th Street, Los Angeles, California 90018,
UNITED STATES
losangeles@sivananda.org
www.sivananda.org/la

URUGUAY

Asociación de Yoga Sivananda

Acevedo Díaz 1523
Montevideo 11200, URUGUAY
montevideo@sivananda.org
www.sivananda.org/montevideo

VIETNAM

Sivananda Yoga Vedanta Centre

25 Tran Quy Khoach Street, District 1
Ho Chi Minh City, VIETNAM
hochiminh@sivananda.org
www.sivananda.org/vietnam

Sivananda Yoga Vedanta Centre

B2-11 Golf Valley, Ward 2,
Da Lat City, Lam
Dong Province, VIETNAM
dalat@sivananda.org
www.sivanandayogavietnam.org